DINOSAUR
IDENTIFIER

DINOSAUR
IDENTIFIER

STEVE PARKER

MALLARD
PRESS

MALLARD PRESS
An imprint of BDD Promotional Book
Company, Inc.,
666 Madison Avenue
New York, NY 10103

Mallard Press and its accompanying design
and logo are trademarks of
BDD Promotional Book Company, Inc.

First published in the United States of America
in 1991 by the Mallard Press

ISBN 0-7924-5513-4

A QUINTET BOOK

This book was designed and produced by
Quintet Publishing Limited
6 Blundell Street
London N7 9BH

Creative Director: Terry Jeavons
Art Director: Ian Hunt
Designer: Chris Dymond
Project Editor: Sally Harper
Editor: Louise Bostock
Picture Researcher: Liz Edison

Typeset in Great Britain by
Central Southern Typesetters, Eastbourne
Manufactured in Hong Kong by
Regent Publishing Services Limited
Printed in Hong Kong by
Leefung-Asco Printers Limited

Contents

Introduction

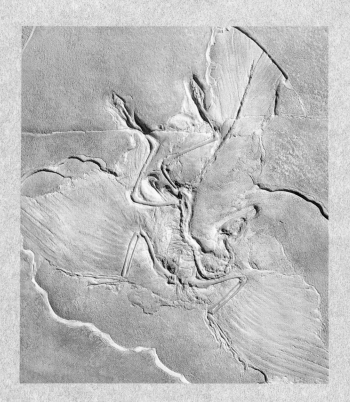

ABOVE One of only a handful of fossils of the first known bird *Archaeopteryx*, from the middle of the Age of Dinosaurs, about 150 million years ago. It had numerous reptilian features, and was so similar to small dinosaurs that one specimen was misidentified for many years as the little Saurischian, *Compsognathus*. Further study revealed its true identity in the 1970s.

*T*he dinosaurs have all been dead and gone for 65 million years, but they still seem to exert an undying fascination on almost everyone. Many dinosaurs were huge, longer than a truck or taller than a house. Many were ferocious to a degree that would overwhelm today's big hunters, such as tigers or bears. Others were armoured like tanks, or fleeter than a racehorse. All were unlike any animal alive today.

Although these creatures were long gone when the first people walked on Earth, they have left traces of their passing in the form of fossils. Using fossils, we can interpret and imagine how the dinosaurs lived their lives.

For centuries, people have been finding strange bits of rock in the ground. These fragments seemed to be more connected with the living world rather than the non-living, geological world of stones and minerals. Stone Age people used these pieces of rock as trinkets, but as far as we know, they did not understand their significance.

Some great historical thinkers, such as the Greek historian Xenophanes and the Renaissance polymath Leonardo da Vinci, suspected that fossils were remains of past life forms. However, religious leaders of their day found such ideas contrary to the scriptures' teachings and did their best to discourage them. But by the nineteenth century, fossil-hunting had become a fashionable pursuit. Naturalists began to make educated guesses at the origins of their rapidly-accumulating collections of huge stone bones. In this way, the fascinating lost world of the dinosaurs was rediscovered.

Naming names

The larger and more spectacular fossils began to be studied in great detail, and similarities to living animals were sought. In the 1820s William Buckland, an anatomist from Oxford, was the first to realize that some of these bones belonged to huge meat-eating reptiles. His M*egalosaurus* was the first dinosaur to be given a scientific Latin name. Meanwhile, in about 1822, the physician and fossil-hunter Gideon Mantell, from Sussex, had found some strange teeth. After

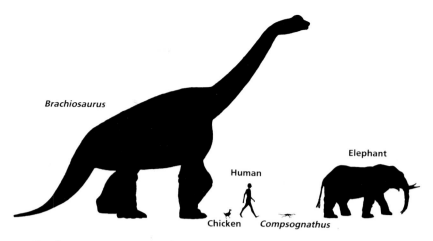

Brachiosaurus

Human

Chicken *Compsognathus*

Elephant

ABOVE The dinosaurs produced many record-breakers. The well-known sauropod *Brachiosaurus* was some 20 times heavier than an elephant, the largest living land mammal – though not as big or bulky as the ocean-going blue whale, the largest animal ever (until the recent finds of giant dinosaurs are fully studied). *Compsognathus* was one of the smallest dinosaurs, about chicken-sized.

BELOW The animals shown in this diagram show the stages which reptiles might have gone through. Note that this illustration shows relative posture and is not a guide to relative size. (From left to right) *Proterosuchus* (length 1 metre) was a crocodile-like archosaur from the early Triassic period. *Euparkeria* (length 1 metre) lived a little later and could sprint for short distances on its hind legs. *Ornithosuchus* (length 2 metres) walked on the toes of its hind feet, with its legs tucked underneath its body. *Staurikosaurus* (length 2 metres) was one of the first true dinosaurs.

much research and consultation he decided that they must have belonged to a huge plant-eating reptile which resembled the living iguana lizard. He named it I*guanodon*, or 'iguana-tooth'.

By 1841 the anatomist Richard Owen, who became Superintendent of London's British Museum (Natural History), had decided that these giant, extinct reptiles could not have been lizards. Their fossil bones showed strange features which necessitated the creation of a new subgroup within the class Reptilia. Accordingly he christened them Dinosauria, meaning 'terrible lizards'. This is the name that still grips us with wonder and fascination today.

Then began a frenzied 'dinosaur rush' to find more fossilized bones for museum displays and scientific study. Both prestige and money were at stake. In the United States during the late nineteenth century, two fossil collectors – Othniel Charles Marsh and Edward Drinker Cope – engaged in a bitter battle to find bigger and better dinosaur remains. They discovered many of the sites and invented many of the techniques still used by palaeontologists today. Their feud greatly advanced our knowledge of the dinosaurs and other prehistoric creatures.

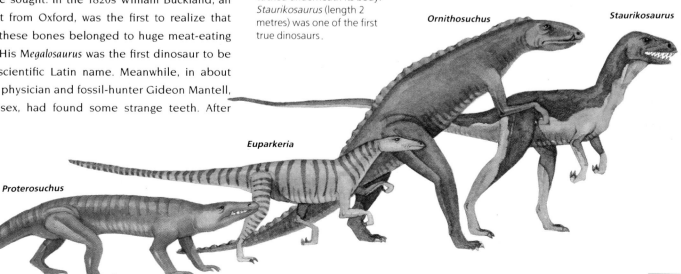

Ornithosuchus

Staurikosaurus

Euparkeria

Proterosuchus

Rocks and fossils

Before discussing the detailed lives and ways of the dinosaurs, it is necessary to understand some of the background to their preservation in the form of fossils. This enables us to realize the limitations of our knowledge and guesswork.

Rocks are formed when incredibly hot liquid rock known as magma, deep below the Earth's surface, wells up and solidifies on the surface. This forms the igneous type of solid rock. Along with other rock types, this is then worn down to fragments by the action of rain, ice, snow, waves, wind and other agents of erosion.

The fragments collect, usually under water, as sediments – the mud at the bottom of a lake or the ooze on the sea bed. Gradually the fragments are buried as more sediments pile on top. Under the intense pressure exerted by this build-up of weight, the structure of the sediments is altered, both physically and chemically. Eventually they solidify and turn to rock. This form is known as sedimentary rock. It is named after the fragments and deposits that formed it, such as sandstone and mudstone. It is usually layered, showing variations in the colour and thickness of each stratum. These variations reflect the conditions of sedimentation. Each type of sedimentary rock is

therefore different and carries a history of its formation.

Fossils are found mainly in sedimentary rocks. In fact some rocks, for example chalk, which formed beneath the sea, are made almost entirely from the preserved remains of organisms, such as the calcareous shells of simple sea creatures.

Revealing Earth's treasures

Earthquakes and volcanoes bear witness to the continual movements of our Earth's surface. The continents sit on vast shields of rock, called tectonic plates, which float around the globe on a sea of hot liquid magma. As these plates move apart, magma wells up between them, forming new rock – usually deep under the ocean. Where the plates meet, the rocks buckle and are pushed up into great mountain ranges.

As the rocks move and buckle, the deeply-buried sediments are sometimes thrown to the surface. Here they are eroded by the action of wind and water to become sediments again, in a continuing cycle of rock production and destruction. The fossils in the rocks are also brought to the surface and exposed for us to find. It is thanks to the rock cycle that the remains of dinosaurs and other long-gone animals and plants are revealed.

BELOW On this world map are marked the sites of important dinosaur finds. Some symbols represent major fossil finds; others show the place where only a small fragment of bone has been unearthed.

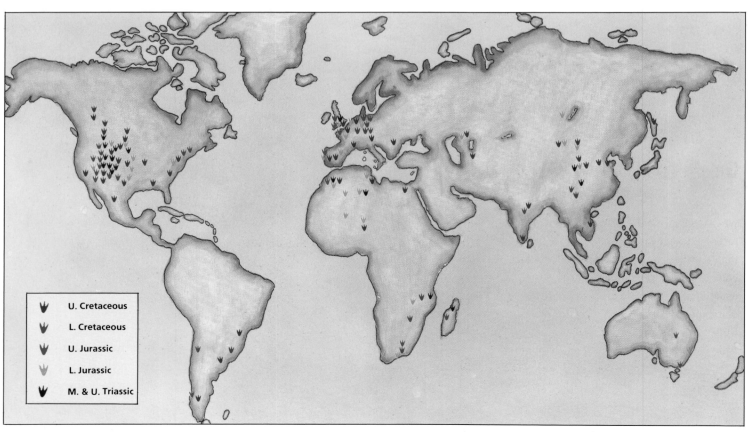

🦅	U. Cretaceous
🦅	L. Cretaceous
🦅	U. Jurassic
🦅	L. Jurassic
🦅	M. & U. Triassic

Fossilization

Nature is the ultimate recycler, re-using the component parts of living things. When animals and plants die they are usually eaten, or they decompose through the action of fungi and bacteria. They are only preserved as fossils when such processes are prevented.

On rare occasions an organism is buried rapidly in fine muddy sediments. Exceptionally rarely, the whole body is covered before there is any scavenging or decay of the soft tissues. This may happen if an animal falls into a tar pit or becomes frozen into a glacier. More often the soft tissues rot or are consumed by carrion-feeders, to leave only the harder, resistant parts such as shells, teeth and bones.

The processes of rock erosion ensure that the remains are buried by more and more sediments. Eventually a great weight of sediments builds up above, producing gigantic pressures which crush the particles together. At the same time water, laden with dissolved minerals, percolates through. Either mineral crystals then form between the particles or the preserved remains are dissolved away and replaced, bit by bit, with rock-forming minerals. The once-organic remains are turned to stone, and a fossil is formed.

The fossil is destined for the same fate as the rock that contains it. It may sink into the liquid magma beneath, or be pushed upwards to the surface of the Earth by crust movements. Here the inevitable erosion of the rock may free the fossil from its incarceration.

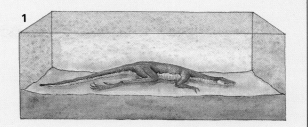

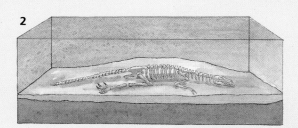

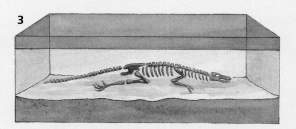

LEFT The process of fossilization. The parts of the animal must come to rest in a place where they are unlikely to be scavenged or decompose, before being completely covered by fine sediment. This is often at the bottom of a body of water, where extreme temperature, low oxygen concentration or high salt concentration 'sterilizes' the water, and there is a continual rain of silt from above. As the weight of silt over the fossil builds up, the processes of fossilization begin. The minerals in the bones are replaced and the fossil becomes rock. Sometimes the bone may be dissolved away instead and the resulting holes, or mould fossils, can be used to reconstruct the bones with latex or plaster. Or the holes may be filled with minerals while still in the rock, producing a cast fossil.

1 **Dinosaur dies and soft parts may rot**
2 **Burial of bones and other hard parts by fine sediments**
3 **More sediments collect, bone minerals dissolve and rock-forming minerals percolate into bones**
4 **Fossil is exposed when rocks are pushed to the surface and weathered**

Geological time: the record in the rocks

When geologists first discovered that the layering of rocks had happened over vast periods of time, and that the oldest rocks were usually beneath the youngest, they gave names to the layers. They were usually called after the place where a particular type of rock was first studied. For example, Cambrian rocks were first found in Wales, and the Roman name for Wales was Cambria.

Because these rocks were laid down during specific periods in the past, one above the other, their names can be used to specify a prehistoric period on Earth. In this way geologists have produced a cal-

endar of geological eras and periods, each dated relative to the next. This is why we read of a certain dinosaur having lived during the early Jurassic, or the late Cretaceous.

When the phenomenon of radioactivity was discovered, scientists found that rocks contained certain radioactive components. Knowing the rates of radioactive decay, they could calculate backwards. According to this, our Earth is some 4,500 million years old.

From the types of sedimentary rocks in which their fossils are found, we know that dinosaurs lived during the Mesozoic era. This consisted of three periods: the Triassic (225–193 million years ago), Jurassic (193–136 million years ago), and Cretaceous (136–65 million years ago).

BELOW The scale of geological time. The planet condensed from a cloud of gas some 4,900 million years ago, and its crust formed as it cooled over the next few hundred million years. At an early stage living cells appeared in the oceans. Multi-celled soft-bodied creatures were abundant by 600 million years ago, but it is only in the last 10 per cent of the Earth's history that the vertebrates, including the dinosaurs, evolved.

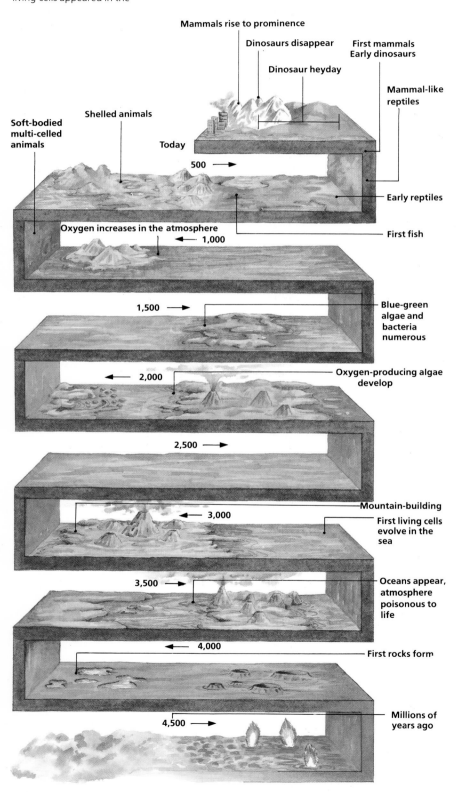

A brief history of life

The geological history of the Earth, then, is written in jigsaw fashion in the rocks at its surface. The different types of rocks are formed under different conditions, and geologists can read them like a book. The history of life is part of this book, and a brief survey will provide a context for the Age of Dinosaurs.

Scientists believe that some 4,900 million years ago a cloud of dust in space began to condense to form our planet. It was another 1,000 million years before the Earth was cool enough for water to appear. But it seems that this water was soon teeming with scraps of primeval life. It took up to 3,000 million years for these to evolve into single-celled and then multi-celled, soft-bodied organisms.

The developing life in the seas changed the chemistry of the atmosphere. By 570 million years ago (at the end of the first main geological timespan – the Precambrian era), many of the simple sea creatures we know today had evolved. Jellyfish, sea anemones and worms of many kinds thrived, although being soft-bodied, their fossils are exceptionally rare.

By the beginning of the next era, the Palaeozoic, some of these animals had developed shells. Trilobites and brachiopods swarmed in the seas. About 150 million years later, primitive fish swam in the water and early plants colonized the land. Some of the fish developed fleshy fins – the forerunners of the vertebrate limb. (Vertebrates are animals with backbones and include fish, amphibians, reptiles, birds and mammals.)

About 350 million years ago amphibians left the water, and primitive reptiles soon crawled after them. By the beginning of the Mesozoic era reptiles of various kinds dominated the land, and the scene was set for the appearance of the dinosaurs.

Dinosaurs as reptiles

The reptiles were the first vertebrates to become fully independent of a watery existence. Their waterproof skin and tough-shelled egg allowed them to live and breed on land. The moist-skinned amphibians with their jelly-like spawn, on the other hand, never lost their dependence on water to complete their life cycle.

One of the earliest reptile fossils is of a small lizard-like animal, Hylonomus, which lived early in the Carboniferous period, more than 300 million years ago. From such creatures as these, over the next 250 million years, many groups of reptiles appeared: mammal-like reptiles, flying pterodactyls, swimming ichthyosaurs and mosasaurs, lizards, snakes, turtles, crocodiles – and of course dinosaurs. Mammals evolved from the same beginnings as the mammal-like reptiles, and sometime near the origins of the dinosaurs were creatures that developed into birds.

Reptiles are classified according to the presence or absence of certain holes in the sides of the skull bones, towards the rear of the head. This classification allows both living and fossilized (where the skull is preserved) reptiles to be studied. The reasons for the appearance of the various holes are unclear. They

may have been necessary to allow the jaw muscles to bulge, or for a greater area of bone to anchor them, or perhaps even to save weight.

BELOW This chart shows representatives of the main group of dinosaurs and when they appeared. We know approximately when they lived, because we know the age of the rocks in which their fossils are found. Triassic rocks, from 225 to about 190 million years ago, contain only a few of the earliest dinosaurs. During the Jurassic Period, until about 135 million years ago, the great diversification took place and the main dinosaur groups appeared. The Cretaceous period, until 65 million years ago, showed continuing diversification before rapid decline.

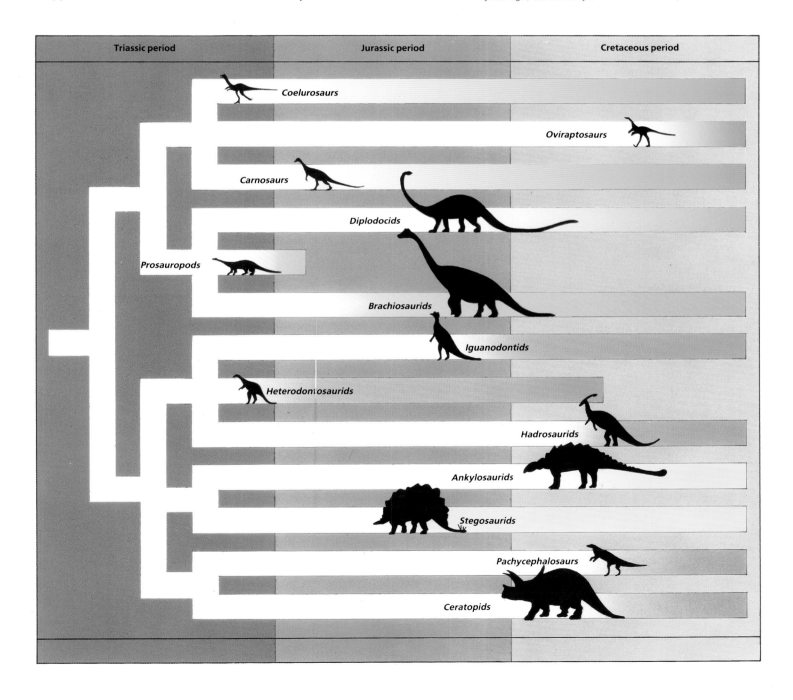

| Triassic period | Jurassic period | Cretaceous period |

Coelurosaurs

Oviraptosaurs

Carnosaurs

Diplodocids

Prosauropods

Brachiosaurids

Iguanodontids

Heterodontosaurids

Hadrosaurids

Ankylosaurids

Stegosaurids

Pachycephalosaurs

Ceratopids

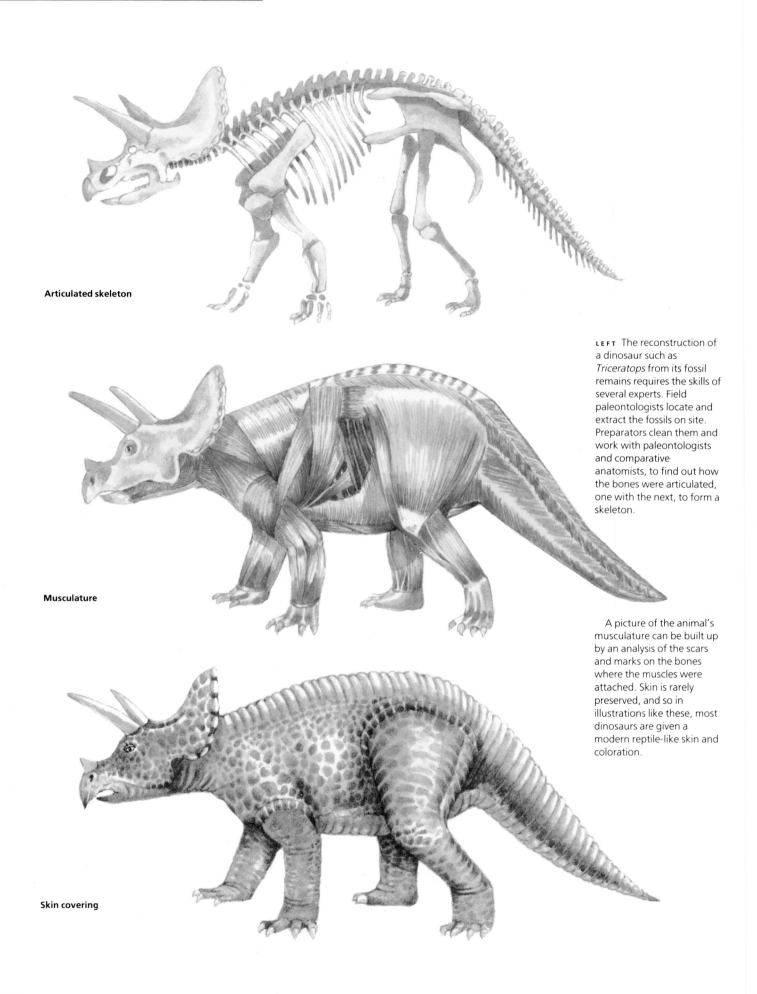

Articulated skeleton

Musculature

Skin covering

LEFT The reconstruction of a dinosaur such as *Triceratops* from its fossil remains requires the skills of several experts. Field paleontologists locate and extract the fossils on site. Preparators clean them and work with paleontologists and comparative anatomists, to find out how the bones were articulated, one with the next, to form a skeleton.

A picture of the animal's musculature can be built up by an analysis of the scars and marks on the bones where the muscles were attached. Skin is rarely preserved, and so in illustrations like these, most dinosaurs are given a modern reptile-like skin and coloration.

Holes in the head

The most primitive reptiles, such as *Hylonomus*, had no openings at the back of the skull. This group is termed the anapsids. Modern turtles and tortoises have a similar arrangement; indeed they lived alongside the earliest dinosaurs.

The next – and extinct – group of reptiles had an opening low down on either side at the back of the skull. These creatures, known as synapsids, appeared early in reptile evolution and were the dominant land animals before the dinosaurs. They had many mammal-like characteristics and early ancestors of mammals are included among them.

Another group of reptiles, the euryapsids, were all marine animals. They included ichthyosaurs, plesiosaurs, placodonts and nothosaurs. They had an opening on either side at the back of the skull, but in a higher position than that of the synapsids. They too are all extinct, and there is some debate as to their exact classification.

The fourth group, the diapsids, includes the most successful reptiles: snakes and lizards, the strange *Sphenodon* or tuatara, and the dinosaurs, pterosaurs, crocodiles and bird ancestors. These animals generally have two openings on each side of the back of the skull. Thus when a new fossil skull is discovered, the pattern of holes can be used to determine in which group it belongs. Similar bone features are used to trace the animal's path through the classification hierarchy, hopefully to identify it right up to species level.

More gaps than fossils

The rock cycle and the processes of fossilization require forces and timespans outside our normal range of comprehension. Incredible amounts of rock and unimaginable pressures are involved, over unthink-

BELOW The diapsids were the most successful reptiles out of the water. The pterosaurs, such as this small pterodactyl, dominated the skies for millions of years and were masters of the art of gliding. Among them were the biggest creatures that have ever flown; they were the size of a small plane.

able periods of time. Finding fossils is therefore a very improbable event.

The chances of fossils forming in the first place are remote, because nature is so good at recycling the components of living things. The chances of fossils being returned to the surface of the Earth, before the rock in which they lie sinks and becomes liquid magma, are again remote. The chances of a knowledgeable person being there to recognize and recover the fossil are also slim, particularly as it is quickly worn down by erosion into sedimentary particles.

So what we know about dinosaurs is fragmentary and conjectural. Our best guesses about these beasts are informed by our assumption that they must have experienced similar adaptation problems to the animals we know today. With our knowledge of the familiar, then, we are able to conjecture about the unfamiliar.

Dinosaurs are perhaps the most studied of all fossils. Some we know well, from many beautifully preserved remains. But most of these ancient reptiles are known only from fragments or parts of skeletons, in various states of completeness. The job of palaeontologists is to clean and prepare the fossils to such a state that the maximum amount of information can be gleaned from them. What did the animals look like? How did they live, feed, breed and die? And what were their evolutionary relationships with other animals?

This book brings the reader up to date with current theories about the world of the dinosaurs. Their world is in the past, and cannot change. But our perceptions of it readily change – new fossil finds are made, as techniques and methods improve, and as already-studied remains are re-evaluated in the light of progressing views and opinions. This constant re-interpretation of how the dinosaurs lived only serves to increase the fascination and wonder they hold.

Origins of the dinosaurs

ABOVE A beautiful fossil of an ichthyosaur, a swimming reptile which looked outwardly like a porpoise, and probably led a very similar life during the Age of Dinosaurs. Fossils provide the evidence for how extinct animals lived. The key to reading them is to compare their features with the equivalent features in living animals, and thereby make 'educated guesses'.

At the beginning of the Mesozoic era, 225 million years ago, the world map was very different from today. All the main land masses were joined together into one enormous lump, the supercontinent of Pangaea. Since that time the continents have gradually moved apart and taken up their present positions. We know that dinosaurs populated just about all of Pangaea, and every continent resulting from its break-up, since their fossils have been found worldwide.

During the Triassic (the first period of the Mesozoic era), sea levels were low and more dry land was exposed compared to today. A greater proportion of sedimentary rocks, which are usually formed beneath the sea, were laid down on land at this time. The types of sandstones produced during these long-gone millenia indicate an arid, desert-like climate. Nowadays the centres of the large continents, especially Africa, Asia and Australia, are dry, desert regions; so it is likely that the huge area of Pangaea had vast regions subjected to an arid climate. The animals and plants must have been well adapted to hot, dry conditions.

Mass extinction

The end of the Permian period, the last geological period of the Palaeozoic era, was marked by an enormous decrease in the diversity of fossils in the rocks. Our conclusion is that there was a mass extinction – indeed, the greatest mass extinction found throughout the fossil record. Many animals disappeared quite suddenly, in geological terms. The dinosaurs themselves and many other animals were to suffer the same fate, 160 million years later.

Fossils tell us that mass extinctions have punctuated the history of life at many intervals. The reasons for their occurrence are largely unknown, but a reasonable guess is that they reflect some drastic change which many animals could not either survive at the time or evolve fast enough to counteract.

In the seas after the catastrophic 'end-of-Permian event' the ammonites flourished rapidly, although they had survived through only one group of their kind. Shellfish such as brachiopods and mollusc bivalves also survived, but many of the other invertebrate groups were severely depleted. From this disaster was born the Age of Reptiles. Although there were many sharks and other fish in the seas, the dominant predators came to be huge marine reptiles such as ichthyosaurs ('fish-lizards') and nothosaurs.

Pangaea

Pangaea

Late Triassic

ABOVE AND BELOW The drifting of the continents during prehistory. At the beginning of the Triassic period the continents were joined together in one huge supercontinent, called Pangaea. As the Jurassic period took over, a rift appeared which became the Atlantic Ocean, as North America moved westwards. The supercontinent of Gondwanaland, consisting of South America, Africa, India, Antarctica and Australia, began to move away from Europe in the Jurassic. During the Cretaceous period, Gondwanaland split gradually into the continents we know today. The distribution of similar dinosaur fossils on different continents is explained by this process.

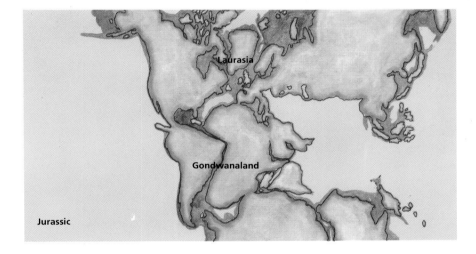

Laurasia

Gondwanaland

Jurassic

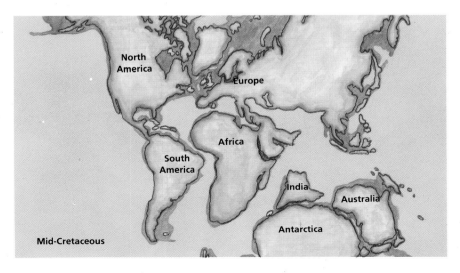

North America

Europe

Africa

South America

India

Australia

Antarctica

Mid-Cretaceous

A flowerless landscape

On land, the predominant plants of the time were the gymnosperms, plants that had no covering to their seeds. They included the cycads, gingkos and conifers. They were tough and woody, they did not have flowers; and they bore their seeds on types of cone. Ecologically, they provided food and shelter for millipedes, centipedes, scorpions, spiders and insects.

Previously the amphibians had feasted on these hordes, but their continued dependence on water meant that they did not flourish in the new, arid climate. As the ponds, lakes and rivers dried up, the amphibians died back. However, the conditions now suited the burgeoning reptiles very well. Some reptilian groups were already thriving as they diversified to take advantage of the opportunities offered. The Age of Amphibians was history. The reptiles were taking over.

Eggs with shells

Reptiles were the first vertebrate animals to lay eggs surrounded by an amniotic membrane. The key to their former dominance on land, these membranes enclose a watery environment in which the embryo can develop regardless of the presence or absence of water outside. The egg also has a leathery, waterproof shell for added protection. Other reptile innovations were a waterproof skin, and more specialized teeth to cope with a variety of foods.

Convergent evolution

We can use the theory of evolution to classify animals and interpret their evolutionary relationships. Animals evolving from one type to another retain many of their shared characteristics, inherited from their common ancestor. Thus the more shared characteristics the two animals have in common, the closer they are in evolutionary terms.

However, nature can play tricks. The forces of evolution sometimes mean that two unrelated groups of animals faced with the same problem, come up with the same 'design solution'. This is called convergent evolution. It occurs throughout the fossil record and can indicate false evolutionary relationships. One familiar example is the wing. This has evolved independently in many groups of animals. Living bats possess wings that look similar on the outside to those of extinct pterosaurs, yet inside, the bone arrangements are quite different. This shows that the wings must have evolved independently.

BELOW One of the most successful groups of reptiles in the Triassic, before the dinosaurs reached their peak, were the rhynchosaurs. They were abundant, though only for a relatively short time, and about the size of a large pig. They had a beak-like upper jaw and tusks in the lower jaw, which they probably used to grub about on the forest floor, searching for roots and shoots.

It is often thought that dinosaurs were the 'first and best' of the prehistoric reptiles, and that other reptilian groups trailed along in their wake. Not so. There were many other types of reptile during the Permian and Triassic periods, before the dinosaurs rose to prominence. They included the herbivorous rhynchosaurs, and also the tremendously successful mammal-like reptiles. These creatures had the same

skull openings (page 13) as mammals and also more complicated teeth than other reptiles. They evolved into many forms as amphibians faded from the scene. Some were lumbering plant-eaters, others carved a living as nimble carnivores. Some, like the well-known *Dimetrodon*, had sail-shaped protrusions on their backs to help with temperature regulation. They were collectively the 'ruling reptiles' of the Permian and early Triassic periods.

The ancestors of dinosaurs and their kin had already appeared in the Permian period. These small diapsids were very successful and today their descendants, the lepidosaurs, are the predominant reptiles – as the lizards.

At some stage there was a split in this line of evolution and larger reptiles appeared on a new branch of the evolutionary tree. These were the archosaurs or 'ruling reptiles', a group which includes the dinosaurs, pterosaurs and crocodiles. These were to flourish throughout the Jurassic and Cretaceous periods.

Dinosaur beginnings

Archosaurs were first represented by thecodonts, who had serrated teeth fixed into sockets in their jaws, rather than embedded in the toughened skin of the mouth as in more primitive animals. They looked similar to crocodiles. They were heavily built, with powerful hindlimbs, and some had bony plates along their back – suggestive of the armour later found in some dinosaurs. Their legs had moved from the rela-

ABOVE The crocodile group stems from the same origins as the dinosaurs. *Protosuchus* was a crocodile that lived in the late Triassic period. It had a wide head with a narrow nose and long legs; it was probably more land-based than modern crocodiles.

tively inefficient lizard-like, sprawling-sideways position, to a position partly beneath the body in a semi-upright posture. These animals continued to evolve during the Triassic period.

By the beginning of the Jurassic period, the early dinosaurs were established. They were lightweight, carnivorous animals. Their legs had moved to a position completely beneath the body, to give an erect limb posture, and they had adopted a bipedal (two-legged) method of locomotion.

The first true dinosaurs were the coelurosaurs. *Coelophysis* was one of the earliest. It appeared about 215 million years ago. Footprints recently found in rocks on a Welsh shoreline are believed to have been made by such a dinosaur. This agile creature had long jaws, and claws on its fingers. It would have chased and eaten amphibians, small reptiles and possibly early mammals that shared its world. This original two-legged dinosaur design was so successful that it continued throughout their evolution.

In the seas and skies

During the Jurassic period, from 193 million to 136 million years ago, the sea level rose and the two massive continents of Gondwanaland and Laurasia became separated by shallow seas. The climate was warmer than today, moist in some parts and arid in others. Conditions were ideal for life in all its forms.

A great variety of invertebrates lived in the seas, where ammonites still flourished. Reptiles had conquered land, sea and air by this time. Plesiosaurs,

Evolution of animals

Evolution depends on an animal or plant surviving to reproduce its kind. This can only happen if the animal or plant is equipped to live in the conditions in which it finds itself. If conditions alter – and they do – then so must the organisms.

Organisms can change to meet changing conditions. Their physical and chemical make-up is governed by the genetic code, in the form of the DNA molecule, that is carried within each cell and transferred to the next generation when the organism reproduces. The genetic code can, and does, change when different combinations of genes are passed to an offspring from the parents. Mutation, or spontaneous change, occurs in the genes as they replicate before reproduction occurs. These changes may render the offspring more or less able to survive changing conditions.

If the organism is less able to cope it is unlikely to survive and pass on its genetic code. If it is well able to cope, it is likely to survive and reproduce. In this way species change, or evolve, adapting to changing conditions. The process is very slow, usually taking hundreds or thousands of generations, but it is also very effective.

Embodied in the phrase 'Survival of the Fittest', the theory of evolution was expounded by Charles Darwin in his book *On the Origin of Species* (1859). Living things have been evolving by this method since life began. It governed the first groups of molecules that came together in the primeval sea. It guided the dinosaurs through their changing world, and it still influences species of animals and plants trying to survive in changing environments today.

It is important to understand the notion of evolution because it tells us that each part of an animal, such as a dinosaur, has a 'purpose'. It is unlikely that evolution shaped a particular feature for no reason. If a dinosaur had a long neck, or sharp claws, or flat teeth, then there was a reason for this characteristic. Many of the design reasons are obvious, especially when we extrapolate from living creatures. But part of the fascination of studying dinosaurs and other extinct groups is discussion about what some of the more outlandish features were for, such as the crests on the heads of the hadrosaurs (page 66).

ichthyosaurs, crocodiles and turtles swam in the waters, while pterosaurs flew overhead. A new group of creatures was just beginning to appear. The first bird, *Archaeopteryx*, emerged about 160 million years ago. It had some reptilian characteristics and some avian. It had a covering of feathers, and a wishbone to strengthen its chest for the stresses and strains of flapping flight, but it still had teeth in its mouth, like a reptile, and its spinal bones continued into a tail. Birds must have continued their evolution after this time, but their fragile, lightweight bones break easily and so their fossils are rare. It was not until after the Mesozoic era that they achieved a short period of dominance on land.

Forests of gymnosperm trees flourished and new land creatures appeared to harvest the insects and other small animals that lived there. The first mammals were the small, nocturnal, shrew-like creatures of about 200 million years ago. They were covered with fur, and we assume that like mammals today, they could maintain their body temperature, so being able to remain active during cold weather. They had good eyesight and large brains. They also had amniotic membranes to protect their young, and these early mammals probably laid eggs. Eventually the embryo with its membranes was retained within the abdomen of the mother, until it was developed enough to survive outside. The young were then nourished with milk from the mammary glands (which give the group its name).

Mammals were therefore around during the whole of the Age of Dinosaurs, but in terms of numbers and variety they could not compete with their scaly contemporaries. They survived and evolved in the dinosaurs' shadow until the time was right, at the beginning of the Cenozoic era, for their rise to dominance.

During the Jurassic period, the dinosaurs came into their own. They evolved from their thecodont beginnings along two main lines: bipedal meat-eaters and quadrupedal plant-eaters. By the end of the Jurassic period, dinosaurs had taken over most terrestrial habitats and were the dominant land creatures.

Dinosaur dominance

During the Cretaceous period there was extensive continental flooding. Thick layers of chalk, formed from the tiny shells of planktonic organisms, were laid down beneath these seas. The vast land masses had split into the continents we know today, and they had

Coelophysis

Classification Order Saurischia, Suborder Theropoda
Age Triassic, 210 million years ago
Measurements Height about 1.2 m (4 ft), length 3 m (10 ft), lightly built
Fossil sites North America
Notes *Coelophysis* means 'hollow form'. It was one of the earliest dinosaurs. A fast-moving bipedal animal that ate small creatures such as insects and reptiles. It had long, narrow jaws with many sharp, serrated teeth, and the front limbs ended in grasping hands.

begun to drift slowly towards their present positions. The climate was mild across most of the world. There was still a great diversity of animals and plants in the sea and on land. Flowering plants appeared and slowly displaced the gymnosperms. Mammals continued to evolve into many varied, small forms.

But it was the dinosaurs that ruled the land. All the famous creatures we know from childhood books lived at this time, including record-breakers such as the most ferocious meat-eater and the biggest animal ever to walk the Earth. There were huge dinosaurs with spectacular armour. Some, from the evidence of fossils, had complex social behaviour.

Everything that is written about dinosaurs comes from educated guesswork based on fossil evidence combined with comparative anatomy. We will never know how near we are to the truth about these animals, but it seems that they lived similar lives and coped with similar adaptation problems to the animals of today. Finding food, escaping predation and producing young were the driving forces in the past that influenced how they evolved, just as they are in the present.

Reptiles, as we have seen, had their origins among the amphibians. The reptile lines of evolution include the turtles, which have remained almost unchanged to the present day; the ichthyosaurs, which died out; the lizards and later the snakes, both of which flourish today; the mammal-like reptiles; and the thecodonts. The thecodont reptiles probably split into crocodiles, birds and the various groups of dinosaurs – the groups we call the archosaurs, or 'ruling reptiles'.

The early dinosaurs

ABOVE *Heterodontosaurus*
was an early ornithopod and
may have been on the
ancestral line of *Iguanodon*
and the duck-billed
dinosaurs.

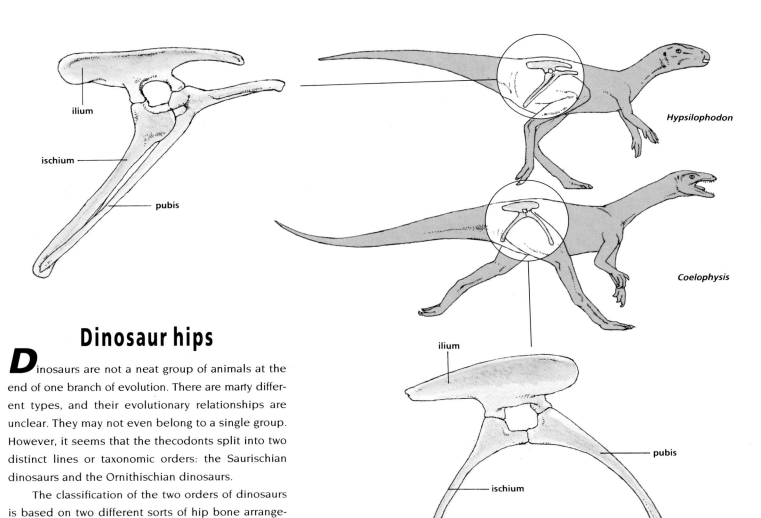

ilium

ischium

pubis

Hypsilophodon

Coelophysis

ilium

pubis

ischium

Dinosaur hips

Dinosaurs are not a neat group of animals at the end of one branch of evolution. There are many different types, and their evolutionary relationships are unclear. They may not even belong to a single group. However, it seems that the thecodonts split into two distinct lines or taxonomic orders: the Saurischian dinosaurs and the Ornithischian dinosaurs.

The classification of the two orders of dinosaurs is based on two different sorts of hip bone arrangement found in dinosaur skeletons. The Saurischian (or 'lizard-hipped') bone structure is similar to that of other reptiles, with the pubic bone pointing down and forwards. The Ornithischian (or 'bird-hipped') pubic bones point down and backwards, alongside the ischium bone, as it does in birds today. Strangely, the birds themselves probably did not evolve from this group but from the lizard-hipped stock; their hips became 'bird-like' much later.

The Ornithischian dinosaurs were herbivorous animals. They had an extra bone, the predentary bone, on the front of the lower jaw. This had a sharp, toothless edge which was probably covered with horn, and it is likely that it functioned like a beak for chopping off leaves. The spinal column was supported by a mass of bony ligaments which held the vertebrae together. The familiar armoured dinosaurs such as *Triceratops*, the 'duck-billed' hardrosaurs and *Iguanodon* were all Ornithischians.

The group gradually evolved to deal with various different types of vegetation, some tough and some lush, some at the tops of trees and some on the ground. Certain members may have eaten water plants.

ABOVE The hips of *Hypsilophodon* were ornithischian, with a long, narrow ischium and pubis running backwards and parallel to each other. The hips of *Coelophysis* show the saurischian hip pattern, with the pubic bone pointing down and forwards.

They had to avoid predation by the meat-eaters and so they evolved weapons including claws, tusks, armour and tail-clubs. Some continued to be bipedal while others returned to a quadrupedal way of life. It is likely that some lived in family groups or herds and may have been sociable animals, raising their young with great care.

Predators and prey

The Saurischian dinosaurs had both herbivorous and carnivorous representatives. The theropods, the meat-eating Saurischian dinosaurs, were mostly bipedal animals. Some were large and heavy with effective teeth, such as *Tyrannosaurus*. Others were small, slender and fleet of foot, such as the coelurosaurs and ostrich dinosaurs. Some of these animals evolved to take advantage of the glut of herbivores, since there were few other predators to compete with them. Others depended for food mainly on insects, small reptiles and similar creatures of the time; their only competition for such food came from the nocturnal mammals of the time.

The herbivorous Saurischians, the sauropods, included the largest land animals that have ever lived, such as the familiar *Diplodocus* and *Brachiosaurus*. This group spans the whole dinosaur fossil record but all the members retained the characteristic 'diplodocid' features, with only minor variations. The design was obviously ideally suited for their way of life, as the shark is perfectly suited to the ocean. It was adaptable in changing conditions, and needed no excessive modification.

Early Saurischians

Both the Saurischian and Ornithischian orders of dinosaurs lost the sprawling gait of most reptiles, and instead they held their legs beneath their bodies. This carried the body weight more efficiently and so the dinosaurs were probably more agile than the less advanced quadrupeds such as amphibians. Otherwise the two orders of dinosaurs had little in common.

The Saurischians appeared first. To begin with they were all bipedal carnivores, and one group, the theropods, remained so until the dinosaurs' end. One of the earliest theropods was *Dilophosaurus*, a large, crested dinosaur from early in the Jurassic period. This animal had weak jaws and probably could only deal with small prey or scavenge meat from carcasses.

BELOW The development of reptile posture. Lizards have a sprawling posture, their legs held out from the side of the body. Crocodilians, such as *Riojasuchus*, have adopted a semi-erect posture with the body being held clear of the ground, but the limbs still somewhat sprawling. The dinosaurs had a fully erect posture, like mammals and birds.

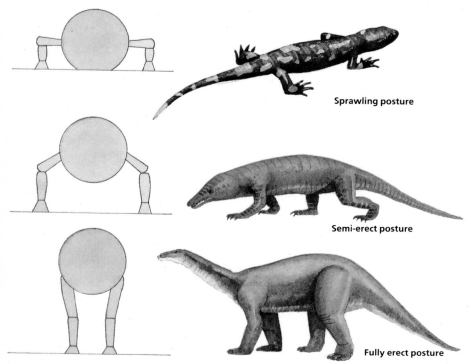

Sprawling posture

Semi-erect posture

Fully erect posture

Dilophosaurus

Classification Order Saurischia, Suborder Theropoda
Age Jurassic, 190 million years ago
Measurements Height about 3.6 m (12 ft), length 6 m (20 ft)
Fossil sites Arizona, USA
Notes *Dilophosaurus* means 'ridged reptile'. This bipedal dinosaur had two ridges running along its face, between the eyes. These bony features were paper-thin but had thickened struts for support. They were probably involved with the mating behaviour of the animals, perhaps distinguishing males from females and used for display.

The other branch of Saurischians, however, returned to a quadrupedal, vegetarian way of life. Even in the early stages their size increased to reach proportions never seen on land before, and rarely since. The first of these animals that we know of was *Plateosaurus*, whose fossils are found in upper Triassic rocks. It could probably move in both bipedal or quadrupedal fashion, rising up on its hind legs to reach high vegetation. Its fingers bore large claws, whose likely use was for gathering and raking down branches, as well as being a deterrent to predators. A smaller version of the early sauropods, or prosauropods, was *Anchisaurus*, an agile animal with short front legs.

RIGHT *Plateosaurus* was an early plant-eating dinosaur. The posture puzzled palaeontologists for some time, as the body did not seem to be balanced correctly for a bipedal animal, yet the arms and hands did not seem designed for walking. However, further studies of the finger joints suggest that the hands could be bent forwards for grasping vegetation, as well as backwards like toes for walking.

Plateosaurus

Classification Order Saurishcia, Suborder Sauropodomorpha
Age Late Triassic, 200 million years ago
Measurements Height about 3m (10 ft), length 6 m (20 ft)
Fossil sites Germany
Notes *Plateosaurus* means 'flat reptile'. These dinosaurs were the forerunners of the giant plant-eating dinosaurs of the Jurassic. They were bulky animals which could walk on all fours or bipedally. They had small heads, long necks and a heavy tail. They crushed plants with flat, leaf-shaped teeth and were the dominant grazer-browsers of their time. They were probably the first ground-based creatures that could reach the leaves at the tops of tall trees.

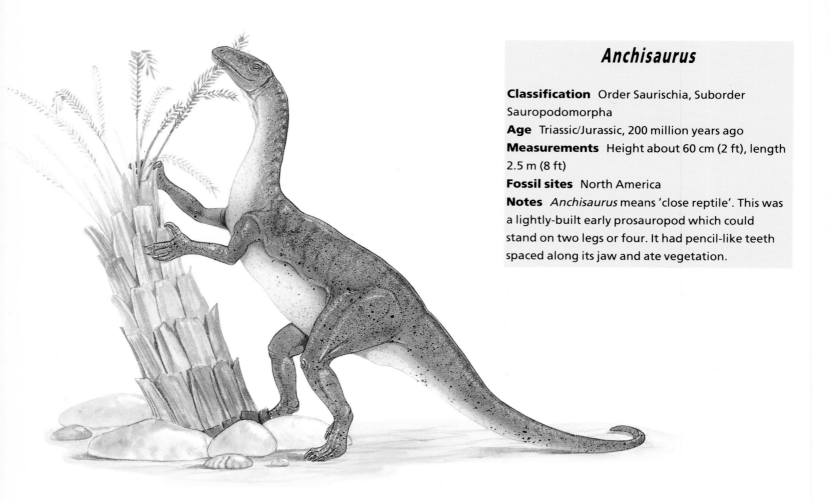

Anchisaurus

Classification Order Saurischia, Suborder Sauropodomorpha
Age Triassic/Jurassic, 200 million years ago
Measurements Height about 60 cm (2 ft), length 2.5 m (8 ft)
Fossil sites North America
Notes *Anchisaurus* means 'close reptile'. This was a lightly-built early prosauropod which could stand on two legs or four. It had pencil-like teeth spaced along its jaw and ate vegetation.

Early Ornithischians

Ornithischians were also originally bipedal, but, unlike the first Saurischians, they were vegetarian. They all showed greater development of the hind limbs than the forelimbs, although some later adopted a mainly quadrupedal way of moving. The earliest Ornithischians were called ornithopods, a reference to the bird-like shape of the hind foot. *Heterodontosaurus* was an example. It was small and agile, and had specialized teeth for chewing vegetation thoroughly. It is possible that it shed and replaced its worn teeth while aestivating (resting up) during the dry season. It also had tusks to defend itself against predators.

Another early Ornithischian was described by Richard Owen in 1859. *Scelidosaurus* was a small, armoured reptile from the early part of the Jurassic period. It was a heavily-built animal, with spines along its back, but its exact relationship to the later armoured dinosaurs is unclear.

During the Mesozoic period the dinosaurs devel-

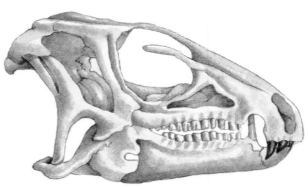

RIGHT The fossil skull of *Heterodontosaurus* shows differentiated teeth. Each side of the lower jaw was in three sections, with moveable joints between. The middle sections moved in and out as the animal chewed.

oped to fill every land-based ecological niche available. They survived on the tough conifers and tree ferns of the forests, the myriad insects and other small creatures that lived amongst the plants, and on meat provided by the herbivores. They were already a very diverse group of animals with very different characteristics. We can no longer think of an idealized 'dinosaur', but a whole range of animals which were as different in their appearances and habits as they were in size.

Heterodontosaurus

Classification Order Ornithischia, Suborder Ornithopoda
Age Jurassic, 180 million years ago
Measurements Height about 70 cm (27 in), length 1.2 m (4 ft)
Fossil sites South Africa
Notes *Heterodontosaurus* means 'mixed tooth reptile'. It had chisel-shaped teeth at the front of its jaw, tusks and broad ridged teeth at the back. One of the earliest true dinosaurs, this bipedal animal's well differentiated teeth and jaws could chew – something only mammals can do today. It was well equipped to deal with the tough plants on which it lived, and its main defence against predators was probably speed of escape.

Scelidosaurus

Classification Order Ornithischia, Suborder unclear
Age Jurassic, 190 million years ago
Measurements Height about 1.2 m (4 ft), length 4 m (13 ft), heavily built
Fossil sites England
Notes *Scelidosaurus* means 'limb reptile'. This small animal was an early armoured dinosaur. It is not yet clear if it belonged to the ankylosaur group or the stegosaur group (pages 57 and 58).

The giant plant-eaters

Sauropod design

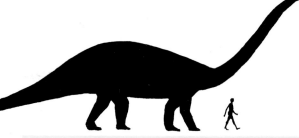

The early prosauropods (page 23) already had the main features of a typical sauropod, or 'reptile-footed', dinosaur. They were mainly quadrupedal, although many could rear up on their hind legs. They were vegetarian, and had long necks to reach up for the foliage of shrubs and trees; the long tail probably acted as a counterbalance. They had long, clawed toes and fingers, and lizard-like serrated teeth.

From this group the true sauropods appeared, establishing themselves by the end of the Jurassic period. The main development was in size. They became larger throughout their evolution, and larger, and larger . . .

Diplodocus, one of the best-known sauropods, displayed the typical features of the group. The teeth remained peg-like in most· representatives. Their jaws were feeble and must have served only for stripping leaves from branches, perhaps with a raking· motion. The leaves were then swallowed whole. There was little or no chewing apparatus – *Diplodocus* itself had only a fringe of thin teeth at the front of its fragile jaws, and the muscle-anchorage scars on the tiny skull and jaw bones show that the muscles here were small and weak.

ABOVE It is still not known exactly why or how the sauropods reached such huge sizes. The largest known land mammal was *Paraceratherium*, a huge hornless rhino of 20 million years ago, which stood 5.5m (18 ft) tall. But it was less bulky and far shorter than *Diplodocus* (shown above), itself one of the slimmer sauropods.

FACING PAGE *Brachiosaurus* only had a short tail because the great weight of the neck was counterbalanced over the front legs by the weight of the body.

Diplodocus

Classification Order Saurischia, Suborder Sauropodomorpha, Family Diplodocidae
Age Jurassic, 145 million years ago
Measurements Height about 9 m (30 ft), length 27 m (89 ft), weight 10–11 tonnes
Fossil sites North America
Notes *Diplodocus* means 'double beam', reflecting the cantilever arrangement of neck, tail and body. One of the longest known dinosaurs – most of the length being neck and tail – this animal was a slimly-built, lightweight version of the giant plant-eaters. It also had its nostrils on the top of its head. There was only one claw on each front foot, but probably two on each hind foot. Some specimens show evidence for a wedge of tissue under the foot, forming a heel to improve walking ability.

Brachiosaurus

Classification Order Saurischia, Suborder Sauropodomorpha
Age Jurassic, 150 million years ago
Measurements Height about 12 m (39 ft), length 22.5 m (74 ft), weight 80 tonnes
Fossil sites Colorado, USA and Tanzania, Africa
Notes This 'arm reptile', although not the longest dinosaur, was one of the heaviest. It was able to browse on the leaves at the tops of trees because of its long neck and long front legs, like a giant giraffe. Its nostrils were placed high on its forehead. At one time it was thought the nostril position indicated a snorkelling underwater existence, but there are no other obvious aquatic features, so this is unlikely. The reason for the position of the nostrils is still unclear.

A built-in snorkel?

The sauropod nostrils migrated during their evolution, from the normal position near the end of the snout to the top of the small head, between the eyes. The reason for this is unclear. It was once thought that these dinosaurs were aquatic animals, and the nostrils on the top of the head worked like a skin-diver's snorkel. However, the design of the rest of the body would not have suited a deep-water existence. The rib cage could not have been strong enough to prevent lung collapse and heart failure, due to the extra pressure of deep water.

However, sauropod footprints have been found which suggest that they did spend time wading in water. The footprints indicate that the animal walked along the bottom of a lake using its front legs only, as the rest of the body floated. The track turns sharply where the print of a hind foot suggests it kicked against the mud. It is likely, therefore, that these animals may well have lived near water, wading and swimming as necessary in search of aquatic vegetation, or to escape predators.

Stumpy legs

Typical sauropod legs were strong, weight-bearing pillars. They were capable of only limited movement, much like our land giant of today, the elephant. They had short, stumpy fingers and toes, only one or two of which bore claws – the others being 'hoofed' or 'nailed', again like an elephant's. As the sauropods became bigger, the front legs grew more lengthy in proportion to the hind legs – indeed, the gigantic Brachiosaurus is named for its long 'arms'.

The vertebrae (spinal bones) were large, in order to support such a vast bulk, but they had cavities in them to lighten their load. In some of the larger animals there were air-filled spaces in many of the bones, as there are in birds today, to make the whole skeleton lighter.

The vertebrae were linked by complicated joints which were strong yet allowed flexibility. Along its length, the spine was designed to anchor the great muscles which the animal needed to move, and to support the ligaments that connected the neck and tail, so that the counterbalance system worked with the minimum of effort and muscle power.

The sauropod tail gradually slimmed down to end in a row of long, thin bones, which must have formed a whiplash that was probably used for defence. It is thought that most of these dinosaurs carried their tails above the ground, rather than letting them drag. Tracks of sauropods rarely show tail-dragging marks. The bones, musculature and ligaments would make this possible, since head and neck balanced the tail like a cantilever bridge.

The long neck

All the sauropods had extraordinarily long necks. Apatosaurus (formerly known as Brontosaurus) possessed a thick neck composed of 15 vertebrae. Each one had fused ribs where the neck muscles were anchored. The longest neck so far discovered was that of Mamenchisaurus (11 m/36 ft).

It is widely accepted that the long sauropod neck was an adaptation for reaching high vegetation; it may also have been used in the water to collect lake-bed plants. It seems unlikely that the biggest sauropods could have spent long with their necks in the tree-tops, because today's evidence from comparative anatomy and physiology tells us that pumping blood so high to the brain would have been impossible for a normal reptilian heart. If these creatures did browse in the high branches all day, then they must have had a more advanced type of heart, with fully divided chambers – which occur only in mammals and birds today. (This is one strand of the argument for dinosaur warm-bloodedness.)

Some sauropods could probably rear up on their hindquarters to reach high leaves. Saltasaurus seems

Apatosaurus

Classification Order Saurischia, Suborder Sauropodomorpha, Family Diplodocidae
Age Late Jurassic, 145 million years ago
Measurements Height 7 m (23 ft), length 21 m (69 ft), weight 30 tonnes
Fossil sites North America
Notes This name means 'deceptive reptile' because there was much confusion about its evolutionary relationships when it was discovered. Like the other diplodocids, Apatosaurus must have fed virtually continuously on plants, either on the ground or in trees. It pulled off leaves with its peg-like teeth and swallowed them whole. Its stomach contained pebbles which the animal had swallowed, to grind up the plant material.

Mamenchisaurus

Classification Order Saurischia, Suborder Sauropodomorpha
Age Jurassic, 150 million years ago
Measurements Height about 9 m (30 ft), length 22 m (72 ft)
Fossil sites China
Notes The animal is named for the place it was first discovered, Mamenchi. The extraordinary neck accounts for nearly half of the total body length, and it is the longest-necked dinosaur so far discovered. The bone structure indicates that it was not a particularly flexible neck, despite its length.

to have used its tail and back legs to make a tripod for such a manoeuvre. The hip and shoulder girdles were large and strong enough to transfer the animal's weight to its rear legs.

Although to us it may seem eccentric and primitive, the sauropod design was obviously successful. It persisted with only minor variations for more than 140 million years. Indeed the same basic format was copied by the other major group of dinosaurs, the Ornithischians. An example was *Tenontosaurus*, an ornithopod that lived during the Cretaceous period. It was not excessively large, but it had a long neck and tail, pillar-like legs, and small hoofed toes and fingers. However, it probably moved more on its back legs, especially when travelling at speed, with the extremely long tail held out straight behind. Its head was proportionally larger than the sauropod design, and it had more complicated teeth which were capable of initially breaking down food before it was swallowed.

Tenontosaurus

Classification Order Ornithischia, Suborder Ornithopoda Family Hypsilophodontidae
Age Cretaceous, 110 million years ago
Measurements Height about 2 m (7 ft), length 4.5–6.5 m (15–21 ft), weight 1 tonne
Fossil sites North America
Notes *Tenontosaurus* means 'sinew reptile'. It was one of the largest members of its group. The very long and powerful tail may have been used in defence against predatory dinosaurs. It had a bony beak at the front of its mouth and crushing teeth at the back, to help break down plants.

RIGHT The skull of the Ornithischian ornithopod *Tenontosaurus* shows that its teeth were designed for chewing, something that the Saurischian sauropods were not good at. It also had cheeks to prevent the food being lost during chewing. *Tenontosaurus* was not as large as the sauropods, since it may not have needed a huge fermentation vat for a stomach.

The ecology of vegetarianism

Throughout their history, the sauropod group fulfilled the same role as major herbivores today, such as antelope and deer. Ecologically, they converted vegetable matter into meat, which could be passed up the food chain to the carnivores.

Generally, animals that eat vegetation must take in huge amounts to sustain themselves. This is because plants are not rich in the nutrients required to make flesh. Meat-eaters, on the other hand, only need to consume small amounts of food to survive, since what they eat is richer in required nutrients and needs less converting. Consequently there has always been a greater proportion of plant-eaters to meat-eaters in any ecological system. In addition, herbivores consume almost continuously, while carnivores eat infrequently.

Plant material is difficult to digest, especially the tough, woody tissue of the non-flowering plants of the Mesozoic era. Modern herbivores have various techniques to break down their food. Cows, for example, regurgitate and re-chew their food (rumination), rabbits eat and re-digest their faeces (refection). In the digestive tract, 'friendly' microbes, especially bacteria, ferment the food inside special chambers. The nutritious product of this fermentation is then readily absorbed by the animal.

The teeth and jaws of ornithopods such as *Tenontosaurus* differed from those of sauropods. *Tenontosaurus* had large jaws, the front part forming a toothless beak for chopping vegetation, while the rear teeth were flat, designed for crushing and chewing. Cheek pouches enabled food to be stored while it was thoroughly processed. How did the sauropods, which lacked these sophistications, cope with food breakdown and digestion?

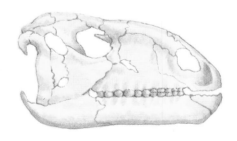

Crushed in a stone-mill

Collections of small, smooth, rounded stones have often been found together with sauropod fossils. One interpretation of this is that pebbles may have been swallowed by the young dinosaur and held in some sort of muscular chamber, similar to the gizzard of a modern bird. The stones could have been used to mash up leaves that were swallowed more-or-less whole. As the gizzard squirmed and squeezed, the leaves would be crushed and pulped, and the stones ('gastroliths') would become rounded and smooth.

The increased size of sauropods may have partly been due to their herbivorous habits. A huge stomach would have provided an adequate fermentation chamber, where the plant material was kept for days while it was chemically broken down in a bacterial 'soup'. The nutritious products could then be absorbed through the rest of the digestive tract.

Defence strategies

The main defence strategy of the giant plant-eaters was their very size. A full-grown *Brachiosaurus* was so powerful and heavy that it would be difficult to tackle, even for the largest predators. However, being at the base of the animal food chain, they must have suc-

cumbed at some stage. Many of the carnivorous dinosaurs were probably scavengers rather than active hunters, consuming the vast sauropods when they died through disease, accident or old age.

Young sauropods, however, would have been vulnerable to the vicious teeth and claws of the fast-moving predators. Sauropod footprints indicate that some of these herbivores lived in small herds of 20 or so animals. They probably lived as a family group. Fossilized eggs have been found, so despite their size, they did not give birth to live young. The eggs and young might therefore have been protected by the huge adults.

Because of the quantities of vegetation that they consumed, the herd must have been continually on the move, searching for new food sources. Presumably they had some form of communication between group members, but their brains were very small compared to the body bulk, and little is known about how they maintained their relationships.

Most of the sauropods, despite the adaptation of their feet to carry weight, retained a claw on at least one toe of each front foot. This may have had a use in raking together leaves, although it might also have made an effective weapon, along with the whiplash tail.

One fossil specimen of *Saltasaurus* shows that some sauropods may have had armour. Its body was covered with hard plates and nodules. Together with the sheer size, this would have given extra protection from hungry hunters.

Saltasaurus

Classification Order Saurischia, Suborder Sauropodomorpha
Age Cretaceous, 70 million years ago
Measurements Height 5 m (16 ft), length 12 m (39 ft)
Fossil sites Argentina
Notes This animal is named for the place where it was discovered, Salta. Although it was largely a typical sauropod, it is unusual in that its skin was covered in body nodules and plates, probably as armoured protection against predators. It had a powerful tail and, like many other members of its group, it could support itself by tail and back legs as it reared up to snatch the leaves from the tops of trees.

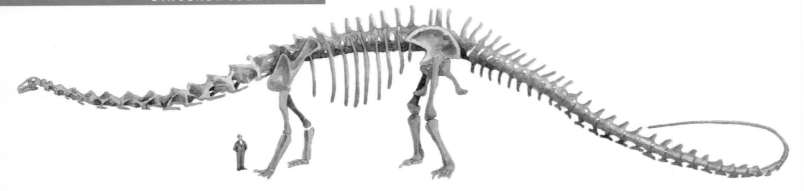

Why so big?

The evolutionary pressures that encouraged the sauropods to grow to such large and inconvenient sizes are still something of a mystery. As has previously been suggested, a large size may be advantageous for the fermentation-vat digestion of plant material, and also for defence.

Another possible advantage involves dinosaur ectothermy, or cold-bloodedness (page 44). Warm-bloodedness or endothermy (meaning 'heat from within'), found in mammals and birds, is very expensive in terms of energy. Large quantities of food are burned to maintain the animal's body temperature above that of its surroundings. The smaller the animal, the greater its ratio of surface area to volume, and so the greater the rate of heat loss from the body through the skin. Shrews, for example, must eat several times their own weight of food every day to survive.

If dinosaurs were unable to maintain their body temperatures above the surroundings, they could have adopted several other devices for warming themselves quickly, and for keeping up the temperature for as long as possible, in order to feed and move about. Their great size would have meant a relatively low rate of heat loss through the skin.

ABOVE A drawing of the skeleton of *Diplodocus* gives some idea of the size of this unlikely animal. The bones of the neck, back and tail were held together by very strong tendons that ran along their tops. The weight of the long neck was balanced over the front and back legs by the tail, like a cantilever bridge.

BELOW *Brachiosaurus* shares convergent evolutionary features with both the giraffe and elephant. The long front legs and long muscular neck allowed the animal to reach the tops of trees, like a giraffe – although much higher, at more than 12m (40 ft), compared to the giraffe's 5m (16–17 ft). The pillar-like legs and narrow ribcage are as seen in the elephant.

The biggest of the giants

The largest of the sauropods – *Brachiosaurus*, *Supersaurus* and *Ultrasaurus* – reached almost unimaginable sizes. The only other animals that have outgrown the sauropods are the baleen whales, especially the blue whale. A whale's mass, however, is supported by the water it displaces. Its large size is part of its extreme adaptation to an aquatic life. It can maintain its temperature (being a mammal) and withstand huge pressures at great depths.

No land animal has been as big as the sauropods, before or since, and there is probably good reason for this. The biggest dinosaurs were at the likely limit of size for a land vertebrate. Legs to support a heavier animal would have been immovable, or would have sunk too often into the ground.

Ultrasaurus

Classification Order Saurischia, Suborder Sauropodomorpha
Possible Measurements Length 30 m (98 ft), weight 130 tonnes
Fossil sites Colorado, USA
Notes *Ultrasaurus* means 'ultra reptile' and it is believed to be around the limits of size for a land vertebrate. It is only known from a few leg bones, but it could have been one-third larger than *Brachiosaurus*. It has not yet been fully scientifically described or named. Another recent fossil find, dubbed *'Seismosaurus'*, could have been as big or even bigger.

BELOW RIGHT The bones of this typical diplodocid front foot show that it was wide and flat, like that of an elephant, and well designed for load-bearing. The first toe had a claw for defence or raking vegetation, while the others were probably enclosed in hoof-like horn. Calculations based on measurements of its fossilized footprints suggest that it moved at about 4–6 kph (2–4 mph).

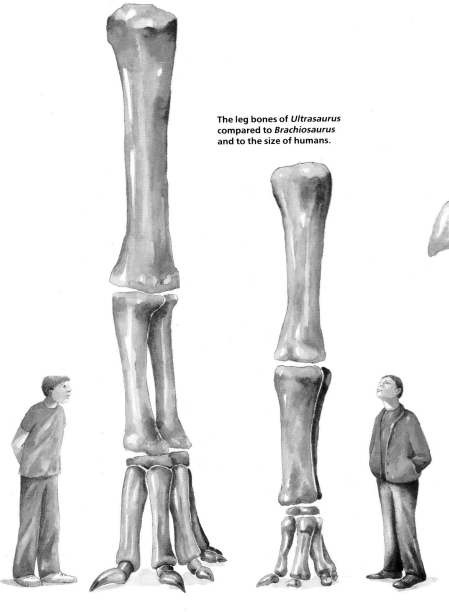

The leg bones of *Ultrasaurus* compared to *Brachiosaurus* and to the size of humans.

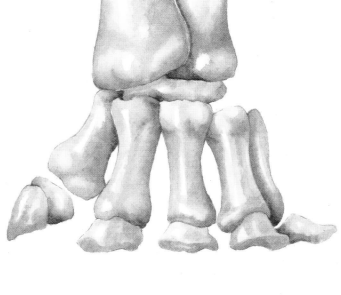

Nevertheless, it has been estimated that these enormous animals could walk at some speed. The bones of the sauropod foot are arranged in a similar fashion to those of elephants, now the heaviest land animals. Biomechanical studies of their movements throw light on sauropod biology. Elephants have a wedge of fibrous tissue under the heel of the foot, which acts in the same way as a heeled shoe, helping to throw the foot upwards and forwards between each step, thus saving energy. It is possible that sauropods had a similar mechanism.

That they ran is doubtful, however, because their limb bones would have broken under the strain. Yet their powers of sustained locomotion must have been considerable, if only to find enough food to satisfy their colossal needs.

The terrible flesh-eaters

Meat is a very rich food, containing virtually all of the nutrients needed for energy and growth. Consequently meat-eaters, or carnivores, do not need to eat as much, or as often, as herbivores. Modern crocodiles can survive for months after a big meal! Meat is also easy to digest. It can be broken down easily by chemicals produced by the vertebrate digestive system; no special grinding or fermenting equipment is necessary.

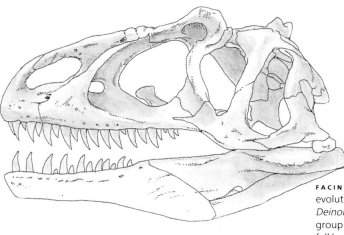

Compared to plants, however, meat is more difficult to obtain. It tends to run away. Herbivores do not need to be speedy or agile to obtain their meals – although they may have these attributes to escape from predators. Carnivores must be able to catch, kill and cut up their prey. They tend to be active animals equipped with good sensory facilities, a degree of sophisticated hunting behaviour or 'cunning', and weapons for killing and dismembering their food. This applies across the animal kingdom, from a dragonfly to a pike to a tiger – and a dinosaur.

The carnivorous dinosaurs belonged to the same group as the sauropods, the Saurischians. The first one to be discovered, indeed the first dinosaur scientifically named, was Megalosaurus, found in Oxfordshire in the nineteenth century.

Like the ancestors of the Saurischians, the carnivorous dinosaurs were all active, bipedal animals, well armed with claws and teeth. Some of them, the theropods, reached huge sizes, although none as large as the great sauropods. They needed to be big, partly because they fed on these even bigger herbivores, but also for the advantages of increased size in maintaining body temperature (page 44).

These large hunters had big heads with sizeable eyes and fearsome teeth. Their necks were thick and

LEFT The jawbone of *Allosaurus* was very deep, indicating powerful jaw muscles used to hold prey. The teeth are also ideal for a carnivore; being recurved, they were efficient at tearing flesh, while the backwards curve allowed them to securely grip a struggling animal.

FACING PAGE In evolutionary terms, *Deinonychus* belonged to a group of theropods which fell between the coelurosaurs, the most primitive carnivorous dinosaurs, and the great carnosaurs. The colour of this reconstruction differs from that on page 41; patterning is purely conjectural.

BELOW *Megalosaurus* was an early meat-eater that lived at about the same time as *Allosaurus*. Its basic tooth shape is typical of the carnosaurs, being long and sharp, with the curve pointing towards the throat, so that meat could only pass in one direction.

Megalosaurus

Classification Order Saurischia, Suborder Theropoda
Age Jurassic, 145 million years ago
Measurements Height 3 m (9.5 ft), length 7–8 m (23–26 ft), Weight 2 tonnes
Fossil sites England, France
Notes *Megalosaurus* means 'big reptile' and it was another of the carnosaurs that preyed on the large plant-eating dinosaurs of the time. This animal was one of the first dinosaurs to be given a scientific name. Its remains are incomplete; many fragments of theropod skeletons have been identified as being of *Megalosaurus* in the past, but further work is suggesting that they are from a variety of theropods.

powerful, their front legs small and sometimes apparently useless. They walked on powerful hind legs, using the long tail for counterbalance. Fingers and toes bore claws but were often reduced in number. This general description, however, hides the many variations in the behaviour and lifestyle of these fearsome carnivores.

Profile of a meat-eater

Allosaurus was a fine example of a carnosaur, one of the groups of theropod meat-eaters. It shows the features and habits similar in all members of the group. However this particular animal was large, and probably too bulky to move at speed over any distance, although it could have been stealthy and agile when close to its prey. In any case, the large sauropods and stegosaurs on which it fed were not fast-moving themselves. They were more susceptible to stalking or ambush.

Some hunting dinosaurs may well have operated in groups or packs which could have brought down the largest of the plant-eaters. But like modern predators, such as lions and wolves, it would be more economical in terms of energy to take young or sick victims from the herds. There is little doubt that they would have also taken advantage of any carrion by scavenging.

The skull of *Allosaurus* was huge – almost 1 m (40 in) in some specimens. It had many cavities to reduce its weight. The muscles connected with the jaws would have been large and powerful, and the jaw itself was hinged far back on the skull, to allow a huge gape. (Another notorious carnivore, *Tyrannosaurus*, apparently had an extra joint halfway along the lower jaw bone, for an even wider opening.)

The jaws themselves were lined with long, curved teeth, reminiscent of steak-knife blades. The teeth pointed backwards towards the throat so that flesh, once bitten, could not slip out of the jaws, nor a struggling victim pull itself free.

Like its cousins, *Allosaurus* had a short, strong neck. This is even more extreme in *Tyrannosaurus*. The powerful neck not only supported the heavy skull but also allowed the animal to twist and pull its head, as it tore and wrenched lumps of flesh from its victim. *Allosaurus* had bony hollows above its eyes, which could have held salt-glands to remove excess salt from the body. Many living animals, such as seabirds and crocodiles, have similar hollows.

Problems in getting up

Albertosaurus was a similar dinosaur to *Tyrannosaurus* but smaller and more lightly-built. It is thought that these great carnivores may have spent time between meals lying chest-down on the ground. This would have conserved energy and allowed them to bask in the sun,

Allosaurus

Classification Order Saurischia, Suborder Theropoda
Age Jurassic, 150 million years ago
Measurements Height 5 m (16.5 ft), length 12 m (39 ft)
Fossil sites Colorado, USA
Notes *Allosaurus* means 'strange reptile'. Its skull was more than 90 cm (3 ft) long and its jaws were lined with serrated, back-curved teeth. Unlike *Tyrannosaurus* this dinosaur had strong front legs with sharp claws on the fingers. It walked on its back legs, which were strong and well-clawed but not designed for speed.

until hunger or danger made them get up. They had strong belly-ribs in the wall of the abdomen, possibly to support the internal organs while lying down.

The tiny arms have long puzzled palaeontologists. They had no obvious function – so were they vestigial? Perhaps, but there are several suggested functions. One may have been to overcome the inertia of the animal's huge head when getting up from the ground after the post-feast nap. The dinosaur would push against the ground with its arms as it flung its head upwards, so lessening the effort involved. The hook-like arms may also have been used by the male to hold onto the female during mating. As with many other dinosaur characteristics, we may never know the true explanation.

The chase and capture

Albertosaurus had massive legs to carry its great weight, but this does not necessarily mean that it could not move at speed. It took very long strides, and therefore covered the ground quickly. Although it was probably not capable of sustained running, it may well have been able to overcome its prey by ambush and short-sprint tactics.

The structures of the skull bones and the joints between them suggest that they were subject to sudden, heavy impact. When this huge running predator caught up with its prey, pounced and snapped its jaws closed, massive stresses would have been involved. The fearsome serrated teeth would have sliced through the flesh, and the lumps of meat been gulped down whole.

Evolutionary patterns

The only carnivorous dinosaurs belonged to the thero-pod group of Saurischians. They descended from the thecodont archosaurs. They first appeared in the Jur-assic period, and evolved into many types during the Age of Dinosaurs. In fact one of the earliest dinosaurs so far discovered was *Coelophysis* from this group.

The theropods showed similar characteristics but they differed in size, and in adaptations for different types of prey. Some were insect-eaters and some ate eggs, some concentrated on the small mammals and reptiles at their feet. Others took advantage of the huge variety of herbivorous dinosaurs around them and followed the dinosaur trend by increasing their size, as explained above.

Tyrannosaurus

Classification Order Saurischia, Suborder Theropoda
Age Late Cretaceous, 70 million years ago
Measurements Height 6 m (20 ft), length 14 m (46 ft), weight 7 tonnes
Fossil sites North America
Notes Famed as the largest known flesh-eater that has ever lived, its name means 'tyrant reptile'. Its likely food sources were plant-eating dinosaurs such as hadrosaurs, and scavenged carrion. Its head was 1.25 m (4 ft) long and the jaws contained serrated teeth 15 cm (6 in) long. These giants may have used their tiny front legs to help swing the huge head into the air when getting up from the ground.

The tyrannosaurs probably evolved from a common ancestor to the carnosaurs, but they are usually considered as a separate group. Their fossils do not appear until late in the Cretaceous period, and they died out with the last of the dinosaurs.

The tyrannosaurs are named after *Tyrannosaurus rex*, possibly the most famous of all dinosaurs, and the largest meat-eater that has ever lived on land. This beast illustrates the general tendency of the group to increase in size. Tyrannosaurs were truly massive. Their skulls were larger and heavier than their fellow carnivores, with fewer weight-saving cavities. The vertebrae of the neck and back were huge and closely articulated (joined). There were belly ribs, as we have seen, and the front legs were reduced to short, two-fingered hooks. The back legs were powerful and the weight was carried on the 'ball' of the foot.

Albertosaurus

Classification Order Saurischia, Suborder Theropoda
Age Late Cretaceous, 70 million years ago
Measurements Height 4 m (13 ft), length 9 m (29.5 ft)
Fossil sites Alberta, USA
Notes This dinosaur, a close relative of *Tyrannosaurus*, is named after its discovery site. It was lightly-built and could have actively hunted prey such as hadrosaurs, rather than waiting for them to die from other causes as the larger carnivores did.

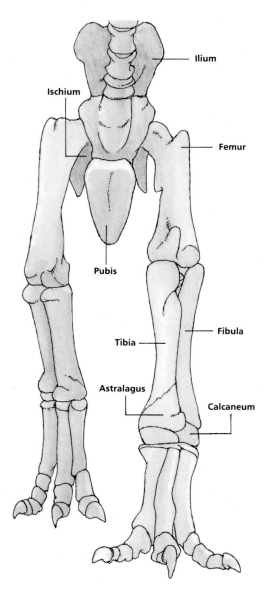

Ilium

Ischium

Femur

Pubis

Fibula

Tibia

Astralagus

Calcaneum

LEFT This front view of the leg bones of *Tyrannosaurus* shows clearly the type of legs needed to carry such enormous weight. They were placed directly beneath the body, a stance that is particularly efficient and stable

Hunting and scavenging

The tyrannosaurs were so large that it is difficult to imagine them chasing herbivores, as cheetahs and hunting dogs do today. However, it should be remembered that many of the contemporary herbivores were even bulkier and could not have run away at speed.

Surprisingly, however, recent studies of the mechanics of tyrannosaur-type skeletons, involving the strengths of the bones and the articulation of the joints, suggest that they might have been able to move faster than was previously thought.

Tarbosaurus

Classification Order Saurischia, Suborder Theropoda
Age Late Cretacious, 70 million years ago
Measurements Height about 4.8 m (16 ft), length 13.5 m (45 ft)
Fossil sites Mongolia
Notes *Tarbosaurus* means, appropriately, 'alarming reptile'. Although it comes from the other side of the world to *Tyrannosaurus*, there are many close similarities. Minor differences are in the skull, and in adults which did not reach the great size of *Tyrannosaurus*, but these two types of dinosaur were almost certainly closely related and probably lived similar lifestyles.

The power of the pack

Another group of Saurischian theropods, the dromaeosaurids, never reached the large sizes of the tyrannosaurs. They were small, highly active creatures. Again, they were bipedal, but both their fingers and toes were armed with relatively large claws.

Deinonychus was a prime example of this group. It had a lightly-built skull and jaws lined with sharp, curved, serrated teeth. The eyes were very large compared to the skull, as were the muscles which moved the jaws.

In contrast to many other ambushing-scavenging carnivorous dinosaurs *Deinonychus* was a hunter in the truest sense. It probably lived in packs which could tackle the large sauropods of the time, such as *Tenontosaurus*. The pack would locate their prey by sight using their large eyes — probably spotting an old, young or sick animal, or one separated from its own herd. They would have chased it at speed for some distance, caught it and clung on with the hook-like fingers. The victim's belly could then have been ripped open as several *Deinonychus* kicked and slashed with their viciously-clawed feet.

Some palaeontologists think of these animals as being slow and lumbering, lazing around and only moving when hunger stirred them. To feed they would simply wander over to the nearest carcass, which they would tear up at leisure. Others interpret them as agile and cunning, lying in wait for unsuspecting herbivores to come within sprinting distance. Evidence suggests that they walked on their toes, as modern fast-moving creatures do, making sprinting possible.

It could be that their lifestyle falls somewhere between the two extremes of either dashing hunter or slouching scavenger. Perhaps the smaller carnosaurs were predominantly hunters, but ate carrion when available. The larger tyrannosaurs, able to catch by ambush the occasional young or sick prey, may have specialized in scavenging. They may even have followed packs of smaller Deinonychus-like dinosaurs and chased them from their catches, as lions chase off lesser carnivores today.

Deinonychus

Classification Order Saurischia, Suborder Theropoda, Family Dromaeosauridae
Age Cretaceous, 100 million years ago
Measurements Height 1.7 m (5.5 ft), length 3 m (10 ft)
Fossil sites Montana, USA
Notes Deinonychus means 'terrible claw' and accurately describes the sickle-shaped claw on the second toe of each foot. These smallish, slim animals were designed for speed, and the tail was used as a counterbalance. It could be held out rigidly when the animal was running, or flexed to allow for sudden cornering. These animals probably hunted in packs and could tackle the large sauropods of the time.

Egg-stealers and insect-snatchers

Some dinosaur carnivores concentrated on the vast walking meals which were the huge sauropods and other large herbivores of their time. Other groups of carnivores, such as the lightly-built coelurosaurs and the ostrich dinosaurs, took advantage of smaller prey. They avoided the problems of battling with and overcoming large herbivorous prey, and concetrated on the little creatures that shared their world.

Insects and other arthropods, such as scorpions and millipedes, were well established on the land by the time of the dinosaurs. In fact they had been among the first creatures to colonize the land, and had already been evolving for 200 million years. Although their fossils are rare, the animals themselves were probably as common as they are today, if not more so. They would have been an important part of the ecological food web, positioned between plants and the larger carnivores.

Another new and important food source was provided by shelled eggs, laid by dinosaurs and most other reptiles, as well as by the newly-evolving birds. These eggs, deposited on land, must have been vulnerable to any animal quick enough to avoid the protective parent or to find them hidden away in a hole or nest.

FACING PAGE *Gallimimus* in the typical ostrich-like pose. It was similar to, though slightly larger than, *Struthiomimus* and must have filled the same ecological niche on the opposite side of the world.

BELOW The ostrich dinosaur *Dromiceiomimus* had very large eyes and a big brain, which may have indicated good coordination rather than intelligence. Its name means emu-mimic and its remains have only recently been differentiated from those of *Struthiomimus*, on account of differences in the proportions of the arms and back, and the pelvic bones.

The smallest dinosaurs

The coelurosaurs were one of the first dinosaur groups to evolve. Their fossils appear in the lower layers of Traissic rocks. The early representatives were unspecialized predators, apparently eating anything they could catch. *Coelophysis* itself, a very early dinosaur, has been found with the remains of young of the same species within the stomach area. Too well developed to be unborn embryos, could these be evidence of the last meal of a cannibal?

The smallest dinosaur so far found and fully described, *Compsognathus*, was also a coelurosaur. One specimen had eaten a small, fast-moving lizard for its final feast, judging by the fossilized bones found within its own body area. The coelurosaur group continued successfully throughout the Mesozoic era, with members becoming more specialized as they developed.

The 'reptilian ostrich'

The ostrich dinosaurs, or ornithomimosaurs, are named for their resemblance – in both shape and habits – to the modern ostrich-type birds. They were a group of theropods which appeared in the Cretaceous period.

Several of their members, such as *Struthiomimus* and *Gallimimus*, have provoked varied theories for their diet and feeding behaviours. The main features of the group include a toothless beak, long arms and fingers, very long and slim but muscular legs, bird-like feet, and a short, counterbalancing tail. One suggestion is that they were wading seashore animals living on small shrimps, winkles and other shellfish, which they found by flicking over pebbles. They might have been 'anteaters', although their hands and arms were not well developed for digging. Or they were possibly herbivores, reaching vegetation with the long arms and neck, and stripping leaves from their stems with the beak.

But the most likely interpretation so far is that these animals were omnivores which, like the ostrich today, would eat virtually any food – seeds, fruits, insects and small mammals and other little creatures – that they could find. The adaptable 'beak' and long fingers may have been capable of manipulating seeds and nuts out of their husks.

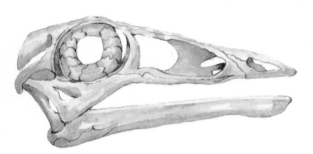

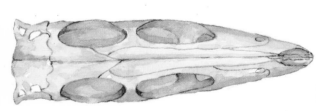

The skeletons of these animals do indeed show remarkable similarities to those of ostriches. They were adapted for speed. The head, neck and body were counterbalanced by the tail. This was usually held straight, but could be moved from side to side to balance the animal as it turned sharply when on

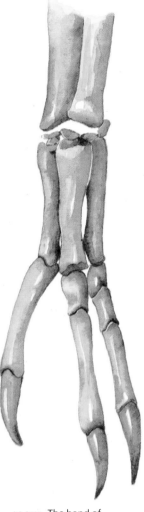

ABOVE The hand of *Struthiomimus* had slim and delicate bones. There were only three clawed fingers, but this theropod could probably grasp small items when the animal was searching for fruit or insects.

LEFT Many fossils originally described as *Ornithomimus* were later assigned to *Struthiomimus*, shown here. The animals were very similar, but come from different geological periods. The skull of *Struthiomimus* shows many parallels to birds: a toothless beak, large eye sockets and delicate bones are all common features.

the move. The long bones of the legs were hollow, to lighten their weight and reduce the momentum as they swung with each stride.

The feet were very similar to those of ostriches, with long toes providing a good grip of the ground when running. Comparisons show that most ostrich dinosaurs must have been so swift that they could outrun enemies, and also catch low-flying insects or quick-moving lizards and other small vertebrates.

Eggs for dinner

Oviraptors were a specialized group of theropods whose likely lifestyle was as egg-stealers (as their name suggests). *Oviraptor* had a short, toothless beak with a short tusk on the end of the upper jaw. The jaw bones and muscle-anchorage scars suggest that the animal had a powerful bite, probably strong enough to crush eggshells. And the first *Oviraptor* fossil ever found was lying over a clutch of *Protoceratops* eggs – very compelling evidence of their lifestyle! The animal could have been literally 'caught in the act' by the processes of fossilization.

Oviraptor had more specialized hands than coelurosaurs or ostrich dinosaurs, with three fingers on each, bearing curved claws. The skeletons of these animals also had a 'wishbone' in the chest made of the fused collarbones. Birds have fused collarbones, too. It is thought that their origins may well lie among the ancestors of this group of dinosaurs, although not oviraptors themselves, because birds such as *Archaeopteryx* had been around for 70 million years before *Oviraptor* appeared on the scene.

Active lifestyle

The coelurosaurs, ostrich dinosaurs, oviraptors and similar small theropod dinosaurs were obviously very active animals. They were lightly-built; their bones were delicate and often hollow; and we strongly suspect that they ate fast-moving animals such as lizards and insects. *Struthiomimus*, as far as we can tell, seems to have lived much like an ostrich – and ostriches are one of the fastest-moving land animals today.

Yet dinosaurs were reptiles, and our ideas of reptiles today are often based on the sluggish behaviour of crocodiles and tortoises. How did these smallish predators maintain an active life if they were cold-blooded? Indeed were they cold-blooded?

There are, today, many reptiles which are active.

Crocodiles themselves can move at speed when necessary. Many of the smaller lizards are exceptionally agile, as are the swift-sliding snakes. They catch fast-moving prey and outpace predators.

But most of these reptiles live in hot climates and keep their body temperatures up by basking in the sun. When their bodies are warm, their muscles respond well and they can run fast. (This is why 'warm-bloodedness' and 'cold-bloodedness' are less preferred terms than endothermy and ectothermy. On a hot day in the desert, a 'cold-blooded' lizard may well have a blood temperature higher than a 'warm-blooded' gerbil.)

Although the small predatory dinosaurs were in general bigger than most modern lizards, it is possible that they kept active by similar methods. There may be no need to invoke warm-bloodedness as an attribute. But we should also examine this intriguing possibility.

Struthiomimus

Classification Order Saurischia, Suborder Theropoda, Family Ornithomimidae
Age Late Cretaceous, 75 million years ago
Measurements Height 2 m (7 ft), length 3–4 m (10–13 ft)
Fossil sites North America
Notes *Struthiomimus*, the 'ostrich mimic', had skeletal proportions very similar to those of a modern ostrich. Scientists believe they lived in much the same way. This able-bodied runner could obviously travel fast, snapping up anything it could find.

Warm-blooded dinosaurs?

One of the reasons proposed for the great success of the dinosaur group is the possibility that at least some of them were warm-blooded, or endothermic.

Birds and mammals maintain a temperature within their bodies that is constant under normal conditions, regardless of the temperature of their environment. Most chemical reactions work better at warmer temperatures, therefore the strings of complex chemical reactions in an animal's body should proceed well at a constant warm temperature. However, extremes of heat could damage living tissue and must be avoided.

Endothermic animals pay a price for their ability always to stay active. They use energy to maintain a constant temperature which is most suited to their metabolism (body chemistry). Warmth is created by the metabolic 'burning' of sugars and other substances in food. The term endothermy means 'heat from within'.

Gallimimus

Classification Order Saurischia, Suborder Theropoda, Family Ornithomimidae
Age Late Cretaceous, 70 million years ago
Measurements Height about 1.2 m (4 ft), length 1.8 m (6 ft)
Fossil sites Mongolia
Notes *Gallimimus* means 'chicken mimic'. These bipedal dinosaurs were slim and swift, members of the ostrich dinosaur group, and they had many features in common with early birds. They had toothless beak-like jaws, large eyes, powerful back legs and a stiff, counterbalancing tail. They were probably omnivores, catching whatever small creatures they could, and gathering suitable vegetation with the long arms.

Ornithomimus

Classification Order Saurischia, Suborder
Theropoda, Family Ornithomimidae
Age Late Cretaceous, 75 million years ago
Measurements Height 2 m (7 ft), length
4 m (13 ft)
Fossil sites Alberta, Montana and Colorado, USA
Notes *Ornithomimus*, or 'speedy bird mimic', was
larger than *Gallimimus*, but almost certainly
closely related and also led a similar omnivorous
lifestyle – even though their fossils are half a
world apart.

This warmth is also prevented from dissipating too
quickly in cooler conditions by heat-insulating layers of
feathers, fur or fat. Overheating is prevented by evapor-
ation of water (as sweat) from body surfaces, by large
surfaces with a rich blood supply that radiate away heat
– as in the elephant's ears – and by activities such as
burrowing or seeking shade.

Pros and cons

The advantages of endothermy include the option of
being active (unless sleeping or resting) at all times
of the day, and during seasons and climates that other
animals cannot tolerate. In this way, endothermic animals are able to increase the availability of a food
source. They can, at a moment's notice, engage in
vigorous activities such as high-speed hunting and
flying. The processes of the brain also work better at
constant temperatures. We perceive warm-blooded

Oviraptor

Classification Order Saurischia, Suborder Theropoda
Age Late Cretaceous, 80 million years ago
Measurements Height 1.3 m (4.3 ft), length 1.5–2 m (5–6.5 ft)
Fossil sites Mongolia
Notes *Oviraptor* was the original 'egg thief'. The heavy, toothless beak, with a horny covering in life, was probably used to break open the eggs of other dinosaurs (or birds) so that it could consume the contents. It had three long, clawed fingers on each hand, and ran like an ostrich or emu on its hind legs.

animals as apparently more intelligent, with consequent advantages for food-gathering.

Fish are mostly cold-blooded, or ectothermic ('heat from without'). Their bodies stay at or around the temperature of their surroundings, and they function as best they can at these temperatures. Indeed, some endure near-freezing conditions.

Modern reptiles do not maintain their body temperature by the expensive use of energy. They passively absorb the heat of the sun by basking, until they are warm enough for the activity needed to obtain food. Their temperature control is regulated by behavioural methods; research has shown that they can do this to a very fine degree. Their bodies can withstand low temperatures if there is no heat source available, so they simply cease operations until they can warm themselves again. They use very little energy and therefore do not need to refuel as often as an equivalent-sized mammal or bird.

Clues from the past

Dinosaurs and mammals evolved at about the same time. In the conditions prevailing at that time, dinosaurs must have had some advantage over the endothermic, active 'intelligent' mammals, in order to become the dominant land animals for nearly 150 million years. For this reason, the idea that dinosaurs were also warm-blooded has been proposed. It is hardly conceivable that we will ever have direct evidence of the metabolic processes of dinosaurs, and

therefore the theory can never be proven. Yet various physical features of the dinosaurs seem to be similar to those found in warm-blooded birds and mammals, and are proposed as clues to the answer to this question.

■ The upright and often bipedal dinosaur posture, with legs supporting the weight from below rather than sprawling to the side, is found in dinosaurs, birds and mammals. There is some overlap, however – certain other reptiles, such as chameleons, do not have sprawling legs.

■ The giant sauropods may have had a fully-divided heart, as found in birds and mammals today, to create the blood pressure required to pump blood from the heart up to the brain, without rupturing the lining of the lungs. This may be true, but it does not require endothermic metabolism.

■ Fossilized dinosaur bones, when sectioned, show a very similar microstructure to that of mammalian bone. This may not reflect endothermy, but the rapidity of the growth of these huge animals.

■ The obviously active lifestyles of animals such as the ostrich dinosaurs imply endothermy.

■ While most dinosaurs seem to have had brains of expected reptilian proportions, some – such as the ornithopods – had much larger brains, approaching the relative brain/body size of birds and mammals; again, such a brain may well have required constant warmth to function.

■ Intelligence levels are reflected in the obviously complex social and reproductive behaviour patterns

Morning	Afternoon	Evening	Night
	Body temperature		
Basking	Cooling in shade	Basking after feeding	Hiding, inactive
Feeding	Grooming	Feeding, nesting	Feeding, nesting

ABOVE Ecto- and endothermy. The lizard is ectothermic, its body temperature dependent on its environment. Temperature control is achieved behaviourally, by placing itself in hot or cold places as necessary. The shrew is endothermic, its body heat produced chemically from within. It benefits in being able to stay active in a greater range of habitats, but at the expense of great energy need: the shrew must spend most of its day eating.

of some of the dinosaurs.

■ Where the dinosaurs lived may provide clues to their metabolism. Dinosaur fossils have been found in areas which would have been near the polar circles during the Mesozoic era. However, at this time the climate was probably much milder overall than nowadays, and without seasons worldwide.

■ The predator/prey ratios of hunting and herbivorous dinosaurs, as indicated by the relative occurrence of their fossils, seem to be more in line with endothermic animals than ectothermic ones. But, of course, the fossil record is incomplete; and new research suggests that predator/prey ratios of modern animals may not agree in the field with that expected in theory.

And so the arguments for and against warm-blooded dinosaurs continue. Further factors include:

■ Dinosaurs were reptiles, and the reptiles we know today are ectothermic. This is still central evidence.

■ Dinosaurs lived in warm climates and could easily have adjusted body temperature by behavioural means.

■ Their tendency to great size would have prevented rapid temperature changes in many cases.

■ They do not seem to have had insulating layers of fur or feathers, although there have been suggestions that close fossil examination reveals some dinosaurs belonging to the coelurosaur group may have had feathers, like birds.

■ Dinosaurs never took to the air or the sea – habitats that the endothermic mammals and birds have both conquered.

Where does this leave the debate? On balance, most scientific opinion still holds that dinosaurs were ectothermic animals. But they were not the slow, dumb, lumbering creatures beloved of old Hollywood films. Many were highly evolved, active, alert, and well able to cope with the climates and habitats in which they lived. Clearly, many of our original ideas about dinosaurs were quite wrong.

Horns and armour

The Ornithischian (bird-hipped) dinosaurs appeared towards the end of the Triassic period. Early versions were small and agile, with the typical bipedal stance of the dinosaurs. They were all herbivorous and continued to be until the dinosaurs disappeared.

Some Ornithischians retained their two-legged gait and depended on speed and agility to outrun their predators. Others grew larger, having developed armour as a means of defence, and then (probably from necessity) took to a quadrupedal lifestyle. These creatures appeared late in the Age of Dinosaurs, and they were possibly at their peak of specialization and variety when they were all wiped out.

of plants, while most herbivorous dinosaurs still fed off the gymnosperms – but as yet, there is no strong evidence to suggest this is true.

Protoceratops appeared after *Psittacosaurus* in the fossil record. Although only the size of a large dog, this dinosaur had already lost its bipedal stance. The increasing size of its skull in proportion to the body, together with the frill appearing over the neck, meant that the front of the body needed the support of front legs.

The neck frill may have developed originally as a bony anchorage flange for the great muscles needed to operate the jaws. *Protoceratops*' cheek-teeth were arranged in batteries and formed scissor-like blades, which chopped plant material rather than crushing it.

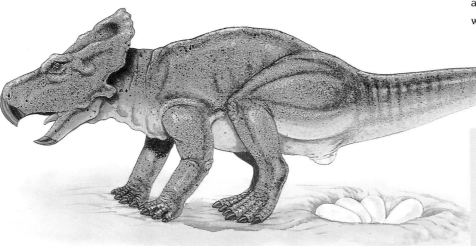

Why have armour?

The dinosaur world was swarming with fearsome predators that overcame their prey either by great bulk and power, or by swiftness and agility. One means of defence against their teeth and claws was to be protected by hard, tough shields, plates, nodules, lumps, spikes, spines and other kinds of armour. The ceratopian dinosaurs and their kin adopted these devices, and in typical dinosaur tradition, carried it to extremes.

The ceratopians were likely descendants of creatures similar to *Psittacosaurus*. This small animal had some original ornithopod characteristics such as bipedal stance and long fingers. It did not yet possess the bony neck frill, a trademark of many ceratopians, but already it showed another of their trademarks: the parrot-like beak and grinding cheek-teeth. The appearance of this type of jaw, not seen before among dinosaurs, approximately corresponds with the appearance of flowering plants (angiosperms) during the Cretaceous period. It could have been an adaptation which allowed these animals to eat these new types

FACING PAGE Despite its resemblance to modern-day turtles, *Ankylosaurus* was about 10m (33ft) long. It was protected with armour-like plating; the bony club on the end of its long tail would have proved an effective defence against predators.

BELOW The skeleton of a *Triceratops*. There were probably several different species of the *Triceratops* genus, differing mainly in size.

Protoceratops

Classification Order Ornithischia, Suborder Ceratopia
Age Late Cretaceous, 80 million years ago
Measurements Height 75 cm (2.5 ft), length 1.8 m (6 ft)
Fossil sites Mongolia
Notes *Protoceratops* was named 'early horned face' because it was one of the earliest true ceratopians yet discovered. This small, four-legged animal had a frill, but its facial horns were represented only by bony swellings. It is an interesting dinosaur because many examples of the remains of its nests and young have been found.

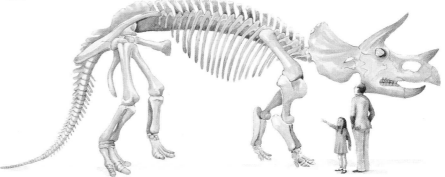

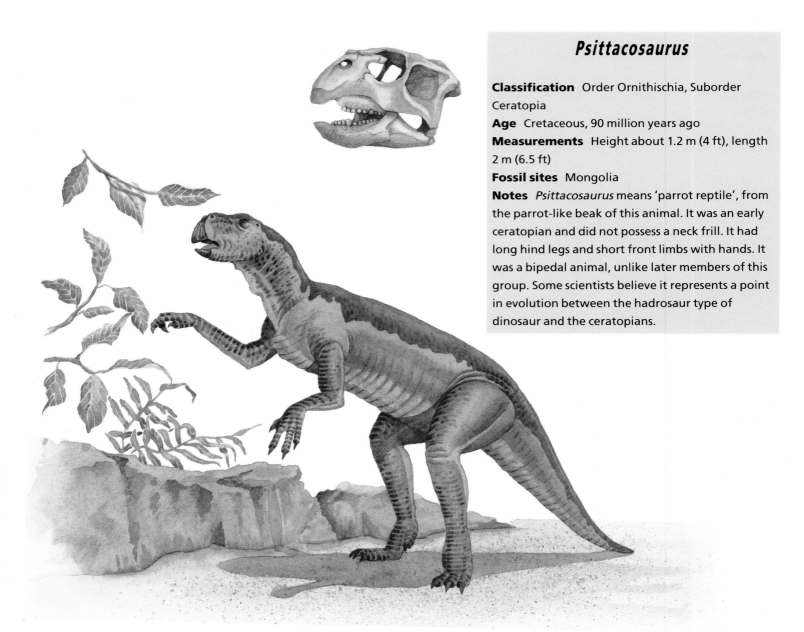

Psittacosaurus

Classification Order Ornithischia, Suborder Ceratopia
Age Cretaceous, 90 million years ago
Measurements Height about 1.2 m (4 ft), length 2 m (6.5 ft)
Fossil sites Mongolia
Notes *Psittacosaurus* means 'parrot reptile', from the parrot-like beak of this animal. It was an early ceratopian and did not possess a neck frill. It had long hind legs and short front limbs with hands. It was a bipedal animal, unlike later members of this group. Some scientists believe it represents a point in evolution between the hadrosaur type of dinosaur and the ceratopians.

Males with bigger frills?

Protoceratops, unlike its probable ancestors, held its head near the ground; presumably it grazed on low vegetation rather than browsing higher up in shrubs and trees. It did not mash its food; and there is as yet no evidence for stomach stones. Perhaps it was fortunate enough to live among soft, lush, relatively nutritious plant food, that needed little chewing to release its goodness.

Although the attachment of jaw muscles seems to have initiated frill evolution, the reasons for its growth to the extreme sizes seen in the later ceratopian dinosaurs, is a matter for more debate. Analysis of the sizes of many different ceratopian skulls suggests that the frills were larger in males than females. One inter-

TOP *Psittacosaurus* showed some of the characteristics of the hadrosaurs, but it belonged to the ceratopian group, and lived about 95 million years ago. The skull clearly shows the parrot-like beak which marks it out as a ceratopian.

pretation is that social behaviour and communication were responsible for the development of eccentric frill shapes and sizes. Some modern mammals have adornments such as antlers, horns, tusks or neck-manes, which signify gender and social position within the group.

Family life

An insight into ceratopian family life has been provided by fossil finds of eggs and young. The differences between males and females indicate a structured society, with males perhaps fighting over, and then protecting, the females and their young.

Many nests of *Protoceratops* eggs have been found in Mongolia. Up to 18 eggs were laid, their more pointed ends down, in concentric circles in a hollow in the sand. Some fossilized eggs have been found to contain embryo dinosaurs, while certain nests also contain hatchlings. Remains of *Psittacosaurus* skeletons as small as 25 cm (10 in) have been found, with their teeth already worn down. Did their parents bring food to the nest, as did the hadrosaurs?

And then came the horns

Continued evolution of the ceratopian group produced much larger animals, with even more elaborate head and neck embellishments. The skull enlarged in proportion to the body. The first three vertebral bones, in the neck, became fused to support the massive

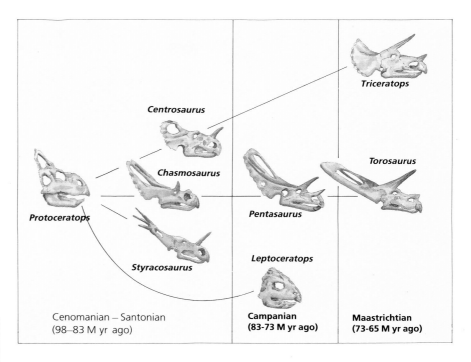

Centrosaurus

Triceratops

Chasmosaurus

Torosaurus

Protoceratops

Pentasaurus

Leptoceratops

Styracosaurus

Cenomanian – Santonian (98–83 M yr ago) | Campanian (83-73 M yr ago) | Maastrichtian (73-65 M yr ago)

ABOVE Ceratopian horns seemed to have been for defence initially, thereafter developing as social and sexual features. At first the neck frill was an extension of the bones at the back of the skull, for the attachment of the large jaw muscles, thereafter developing for protection. From *Protoceratops*, which had a small frill and nose ridge, these characteristics followed different lines of evolution.

weight of the head. The neck frills got larger – and horns appeared.

Centrosaurus had a small neck frill with 'windows' for the attachment of jaw muscles. In these animals the purpose of the frill was probably still mainly for jaw muscle attachment, and perhaps as a visual signal for social interactions. The *Centrosaurus* also had a horn on its nose and two horns pointing forwards on the top of the frill.

Triceratops had a longer frill which had lost the windows. The solid slab of bone had only two slots for the passage of jaw muscles. This beast, well known

Triceratops

Classification Order Ornithischia, Suborder Ceratopia

Age Late Cretaceous, 70 million years ago

Measurements Height 4 m (13 ft), length 9 m (30 ft), weight 5-6 tonnes

Fossil sites North America

Notes The well-known *Triceratops*, or 'three-horned face', was one of the last surviving dinosaurs. The two eyebrow horns on its face may have been well over 1 m (3 ft) long in life, while the skull from the nose to the end of the neck frill measured 3.5 m (11.5 ft). The animal was large and heavy but could probably move at speed and charge to defend itself, in the manner of its similarly-armed modern equivalent, the rhinoceros.

Young *Triceratops* compared to rhinoceros; an adult would be about twice the size of a modern rhino.

from many fossil finds (the large plates and flanges of bone were excellent candidates for fossilization), had one nose horn and two brow horns. This frill seems less for the attachment of jaw muscles, and social behaviour, than for defence against the tyrannosaurs of the time. We can picture these large, heavily-built animals living in family groups or herds, and forming a circle when danger threatened, with females and young in the middle and bulls on the edge.

Although bulky, *Triceratops* could probably have moved at speed for short distances; when provoked it would charge, bringing the nose horn up to slash

BELOW The skull of *Triceratops*. The short nose horn and two long brow horns would have been longer than shown here, since in life they were doubtless covered with horn, a substance that rarely fossilizes.

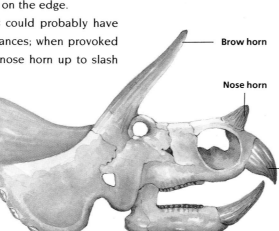

Brow horn

Nose horn

Beak-like front to jaws

Centrosaurus

Classification Order Ornithischia, Suborder Ceratopia
Age Late Cretaceous, 80 million years ago
Measurements Height 2.3 m (7.8 ft), length 6 m (20 ft)
Fossil sites North America
Notes *Centrosaurus* means 'sharp point reptile'. This animal had one nose horn, and its neck frill was edged with spines, two of which pointed down towards the face. It probably lived in small herds, the males defending the females and young.

the underbelly of any predator standing over it. The solid frill would prevent the teeth of the carnivore grabbing lumps of flesh.

As mentioned above, ceratopians may also have used their horns and frills for battles between males wanting to amass a harem of females. The horns could have been locked in battle, but fatal wounding would have been prevented by the frill – and perhaps by social conventions seen in such struggles today, where the loser signifies defeat and is allowed to retreat without further harm.

The frills got even larger. *Torosaurus* was the record-holder, with the biggest skull of virtually any land vertebrate. It lived right at the end of the Cretaceous period, and its frill had only small windows and no notable decorations. There were three horns on its face, those on the brow being as much as 1.5 m (5 ft) long when covered with the horny sheath.

The smallest brains

The stegosaurs were another group of Ornithischian dinosaurs, which appeared long before the ceratopians. They had also returned to using four feet for locomotion. These herbivores varied greatly in size, and they are famous as the dinosaurs with huge bony plates arranged along the back.

ABOVE The splayed spines on the tail end of the *Stegosaurus* would have been effective weapons as the tail thrashed from side to side.

Typical stegosaur features included a small head held close to the ground on a short neck, weak jaws with small cheek teeth (they may have relied on stomach stones and large fermenting gut-chambers to aid digestion), short but strong front legs, and longer hind legs. They had elephant-like feet with hoofed toes. The tail was short for a dinosaur, and ended with several bony spikes – the only apparent means of defence. The vertebrae and ribs were very large, in order to support the great weight of the animal.

Torosaurus

Classification Order Ornithischia, Suborder Ceratopia
Age Late Cretaceous, 70 million years ago
Measurements Height 3.6 m (12 ft), length 7.6 m (25 ft)
Fossil sites North America
Notes *Torosaurus*, the 'bull reptile', is only known from remains of its head, which had the largest neck frill of all ceratopians. The frill was much longer than the skull, itself up to 2.6m (8.5 ft) and one of the largest skulls of any known land animal. One specimen of *Torosaurus* shows signs of what is thought to be bone cancer.

Stegosaurus

Classification Order Ornithischia, Suborder Stegosauria
Age Jurassic, 150 million years ago
Measurements Height 4.7 m (15.7 ft), length 6–7.5 m (20–24.6 ft)
Fossil sites North America
Notes *Stegosaurus* means 'roofed reptile'. Although there are many good specimens of this animal, nobody is still absolutely sure how the back plates were arranged or what their function was. They were probably in two upright rows, staggered slightly, and were most likely used for temperature regulation. The animal would stand side-on to the sun when it needed to warm itself, and end-on in a breeze or in the shade when it was too hot. It used the spines on its tail for defence.

Stegosaurs in general, and *Stegosaurus* in particular, are noted for the very small size of the brain in proportion to the body. *Stegosaurus* also had an enlargement of the spinal cord in its hip region, often called a 'second brain'. In fact the brain in the skull was probably adequate for its placid, browsing existence; the enlargement in the hips may merely have been the place where all the nerves of the legs and tail entered the spinal cord.

Casts of the insides of *Stegosaurus* skulls indicate that the brain of this creature probably weighed less than 100 g (3.5 oz). With a body weight of some 1.5 tonnes (tons), this gives a body:brain ratio of 15,000:1. In ourselves the same ratio is about 40–50:1. Yet stegosaurs survived for tens of millions of years, so evidently the attributes of a large brain were not important in its world.

BELOW The skeleton of a *Stegosaurian* suggests it was a heavy, slow-moving animal, with the massive hind legs taking most of the body weight. This interpretation of the stegosaurian skeletal structure has been superceded by recent reconstructions.

Stegosaur radiators

Interpretation of fossil remains shows that the back plates of stegosaurs were made of sheets of bone held in the muscles and skin of the back, above the backbone itself. Early reconstructions had them lying flat across the back of the animal, like tiles on a roof (hence the name *Stegosaurus*, meaning 'roofed reptile'), to offer protection from predators of the day.

But further study suggests that the plates were not designed to do this. They were probably held up straight, arranged alternately in two rows along the back, each plate overlapping slightly with two in the adjacent row.

The fossil plates are covered with channels, where blood vessels once ran beneath the skin; and the bone itself is not solid but has a honeycomb-like structure. Tests in wind tunnels demonstrate that the plates were ideally shaped to act as heat dissipators in a light breeze. In other words, the stegosaur may well have used the plates like a car radiator, to get rid of excess body heat when it became too warm. And when the dinosaur turned sideways to the sun, the plates would have served as solar panels, absorbing heat to warm the blood when it became too cool.

The plates, then, were probably not for defence, but for temperature regulation. They could act as radiators, giving out heat, and also solar panels, absorbing it. In this way the stegosaurs may have been able to maintain a relatively constant body temperature, at least during the daytime.

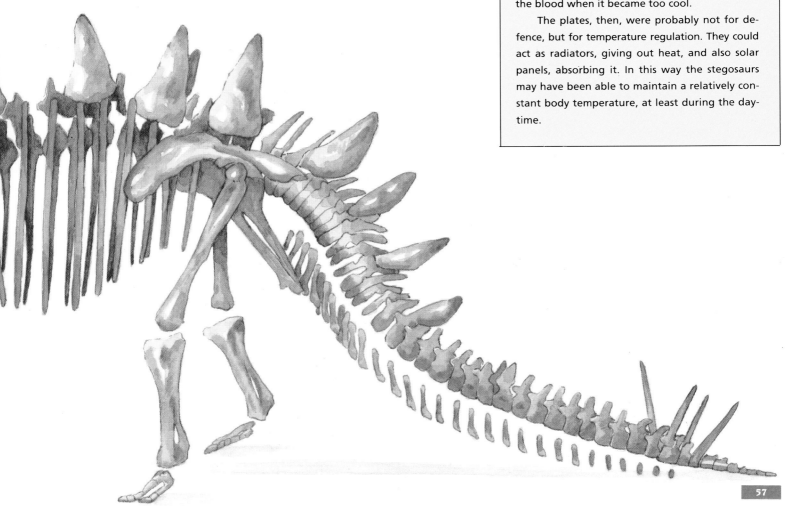

Nodosaurus

Classification Order Ornithischia, Suborder Ankylosauria
Age Cretaceous, 95 million years ago
Measurements Height 1.8 m (6 ft), length 5.5 m (18 ft)
Fossil sites North America
Notes *Nodosaurus* means 'lumpy reptile' and refers to the armouring on the skin. There were rows of bony nodules, alternately large and small, arranged across the back, neck and tail. These animals must have protected themselves by crouching low to the ground like an armadillo, presenting only the upper armoured surface to an attacker, with their shape and weight making them difficult to turn over.

Nobbles and nodules

The nodosaurs and ankylosaurs are two further groups of Ornithischian dinosaurs that developed the armour theme. They were not particularly large dinosaurs, but their skin was covered with various patterns of bony nodules, plates and spines – they were truly armoured dinosaurs.

Built along the same lines as the ceratopians, they had small heads which were heavily plated with extra bone. There was a bony palate between the mouth and nasal cavity, an unusual feature for a reptile, which allowed the animal to breathe and chew at the same time. This was taken even further in the ankylosaurs, which had long nasal passages associated with well-developed olfactory lobes (smell centres) in the brain. They may have used their powerful sense of smell to search for food or avoid predators.

The bony nodules of *Nodosaurus* functioned rather like a coarse chain-mail suit, providing protection and flexibility. *Polacanthus* (a nodosaur) and *Ankylosaurus* had spikes, and the latter possessed a massive club at the end of its stiffened tail – a supremely effective defensive weapon.

These animals were not large, and were probably fairly agile compared to the huge meat-eating theropods. As a last resort, when being attacked, they may have crouched close to the ground, thereby being very awkward to tip up or turn over. The attacker, its teeth slipping and scrabbling on the back armour, may have given up in favour of easier prey. The same sort of defensive behaviour is seen in some modern-day creatures, such as the hedgehog or the echidna. If it came to an open fight, the tail club of an ankylosaur could easily have floored a bipedal theropod, perhaps breaking its leg at the same time – in the same way that a small child, being forced into action, might kick a larger one in the shin before running off!

Polacanthus

Classification Order Ornithischia, Suborder Ankylosauria
Age Cretaceous, 120 million years ago
Measurements Height 1 m (3.3 ft), length 4 m (13 ft)
Fossil sites England
Notes The name *Polacanthus*, 'like many spikes', refers to the spines that were found at the rear of the skeleton. Few dinosaurs have been found in a good state of preservation, so their armour arrangement is not fully understood. This dinosaur appears to have been covered with skin armed with bony nodules over its hip region.

Ankylosaurus

Classification Order Ornithischia, Suborder Ankylosauria
Age Late Cretaceous, 70 million years ago
Measurements Height about 3 m (10 ft), length 10 m (33 ft)
Fossil sites North America
Notes *Ankylosaurus* means 'fused reptile' and refers to the fused body elements of the armour-plating. It was one of the largest dinosaurs of the ankylosaur group. The bony plates in the skin at the end of the tail are enlarged and fused, both together and to the end bones of the tail. This huge bony club, at the end of an otherwise flexible and powerful tail, would have been an effective defence. The ankylosaur could easily have damaged a tyrannosaur's legs, rendering it helpless.

BELOW Pachycephalosaur remains are rare fossils, these dinosaurs being known only by their teeth for half a century. More recent finds include several skull fragments, but little of the body skeleton. This is the skull of *Prenocephale*, which lived about 70 million years ago. It was some 2m (nearly 7ft) long, and its fossils come from North America.

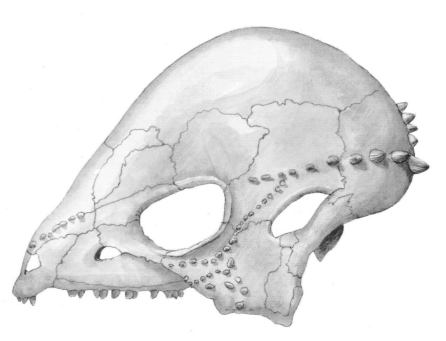

The head-banger dinosaurs

The pachycephalosaurs were another group of Ornithischians, from late in the Age of Dinosaurs. They had not lost their bipedal stance and retained teeth at the front of their jaws. They were mostly smallish, although *Pachycephalosaurus* itself reached great size, being as long as a 24-seater bus.

These dinosaurs were grazing animals and may have lived as sheep and goats do today. They had no armour except for an immensely strengthened skull dome, with the bone being up to 25 cm (10 in) thick in *Pachycephalosaurus*, and small bony knobs and horns surrounding it. It has been suggested that these 'dome-heads' or 'thick-heads' may have defended themselves, their territories, mates or offspring, by a display of head-butting – as rams do nowadays. The fact that the head was held at an angle to the spine, unlike other dinosaurs, and the bones of the neck were thickened and closely jointed to absorb shock, are further evidence for this feature of their lifestyle.

Pachycephalosaurus

Classification Order Ornithischia, Suborder Pachycephalosauria
Age Late Cretaceous, 70 million years ago
Measurements Height 5.4 m (18 ft), length 8 m (26 ft)
Fossil sites North America
Notes *Pachycephalosaurus* is the 'thick-headed reptile', referring not to its supposed intelligence but to the thick bone of the upper skull. It was the largest of its group and, along with the thickened bones on the top of the skull, there were bony nodules and spines around the dome. The curious shape of the head, together with the arrangement of the neck and back bones, suggests that these animals could hold their bodies straight and horizontal, with the head at a right angle and the face looking straight down. In this posture they engaged in charging and head-butting behaviour, possibly connected with territory and courtship disputes as well as defence.

RIGHT *Stegoceras* was a medium-sized pachycephalosaur, about 2m (6.5ft) in height. Their very thick skulls were probably used in territorial defence, or in mating competitions of head-butting.

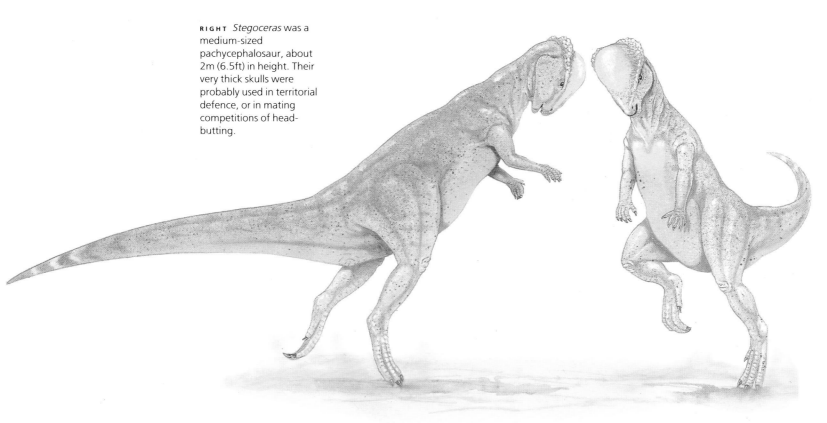

Lizard-teeth and duck-bills

The last main groups of Ornithischians in our dinosaur survey are the iguanodontids and hadrosaurs. They were thought to be closely related, both being bipedal herbivores that reached medium-to-large sizes. They had multipurpose hands and, as they evolved, fossils indicate that there was increased adaptation towards a sociable way of life.

The first of the iguanodontids, *Camptosaurus*, appeared at the end of the Jurassic period, some 140 million years ago. It seems that the group replaced the giant sauropods as the main herbivores around this time, and they continued as such throughout the Cretaceous period. Their appearance and diversification in the fossil record corresponds approximately to the evolution of flowering plants, and this new food source may have contributed to their diet.

The hadrosaurs did not evolve until later, about 100 million years ago. They were becoming ever more specialized and diversified when the Age of Dinosaurs was suddenly terminated, 65 million years ago.

Iguanodon discovered

Iguanodon was one of the first dinosaurs to be discovered to science, and its fossils were extensively studied when the science of palaeontology was in its infancy. Fossilized teeth, and later bones, were found by Gideon Mantell in the early 1820s. He went to great lengths to discover what sort of animal they came from. Great comparative anatomists of the time, including William Buckland and Baron Georges Cuvier, examined the teeth and dismissed their significance, but Mantell did not agree with their conclusions. He eventually realized that the teeth were similar, although much larger, to those of the living iguana lizard.

FACING PAGE The skeleton of *Iguanodon*. It was a large animal with massive hind legs and a heavy tail.

He therefore named his creature *Iguanadon* ('iguana tooth'), and published a description and reconstruction of the animal.

Since that time many complete specimens of *Iguanadon* have been found across Europe and Asia. It is probably one of the most studied of all dinosaurs, and much has been conjectured about its appearance and lifestyle. However, this extensive body of knowledge and guesswork serves to illustrate how much we will never know about life in the past – very little can be gleaned about the beast's internal anatomy of soft tissues such as the gut, excretory and reproductive organs, and virtually nothing about the metabolism. Suggestions have been made by various scientists concerning the ecology and behaviour of these animals, based on studies of the fossilized teeth and bones, and also on the circumstantial evidence of which fossils have been found together, but these will of necessity remain educated proposals.

Camptosaurus

Classification Order Ornithischia, Suborder Ornithopoda
Age Late Jurassic, 140 million years ago
Measurements Height 3.6 m (12 ft), length 5–7 m (16–23 ft)
Fossil sites North America
Notes *Camptosaurus* means 'flexible reptile'. It was a small iguanodont-type dinosaur which appeared early in the group's evolution. It still had four toes on its back feet and no thumb-spike, but otherwise it was very similar to *Iguanodon*.

Iguanodon

Classification Order Ornithischia, Suborder Ornithopoda
Age Cretaceous, 120 million years ago
Measurements Height 5 m (16 ft), length 10 m (33 ft)
Fossil sites Europe, North Africa and Asia
Notes *Iguanodon* is one of the first- and best-studied of dinosaurs, named for the resemblance of its teeth to those of an iguana. It was a large plant-eating animal which could stand on its hind legs. It had a large thumb-spike for raking together vegetation or for defence; the little finger was flexible and may have been used to manipulate food; while the three middle fingers were robust and hoofed for walking on all fours.

Chewing comes to the fore

Iguanadon was a large animal, as tall and long as a heavy-duty truck, although with a weight of around two tonnes (tons). It had a large, narrow head and shortish neck. The front of the jaws was a toothless, horn-covered beak. At the back of the jaws there were many chewing cheek teeth arranged in parallel rows.

The mechanism of chewing was novel and may have been responsible for the success of these animals. The teeth in the upper jaw came down slightly to the outside of the lower teeth, rather than straight down on to them. As the teeth came together the bones of the upper jaw probably moved apart slightly, so that the working surfaces of the teeth could grind across each other. The food was contained in cheek pouches, just as in ourselves, so that it could be repeatedly remashed and reground, before being swallowed.

Iguanodon's brain was large, for a reptile, and it seems that these animals had well-developed senses. They could have been capable of the learning and reasoning processes necessary for social behaviour and care of the young.

The arms of Iguanodon were long and strong, ending in a hand with five fingers. The thumb bore a large spike, which may have been a defensive weapon and/ or feeding tool. The three middle fingers were short and hoofed, and the joint anatomy indicates that they could be bent back upon themselves for weight-bearing, when the animal walked on all fours. The little finger was long and flexible, and may have been used to manipulate food.

The hind legs were pillar-like, each ending in a three-toed foot. In life, the backbone's likely position

RIGHT AND BELOW The foot of Iguanodon had three strong, widely splayed toes. The three middle fingers of the hand could support some weight when necessary, while the thumb spike and little finger may have been used for manipulating food.

Foot

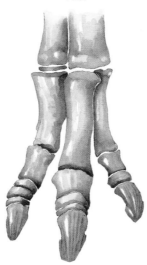

Hand

was horizontal to the ground as the creature strode around. Anchorage marks point to the spines of the vertebrae between the shoulders and near the end of the tail being held together by a bony latticework of ligaments, with parts of the ligaments having fossilized. The tail was heavy, to counterbalance the rest of the body over the hips, and was probably held out behind.

Ouranosaurus was a similar animal to Iguanodon, although it appeared some 20 million years later. Its vertebral spines were elongated to form the supports for a skin 'sail' that ran down the back, between the shoulders and the end of the tail. Richly supplied with blood vessels, this was probably a temperature-regulating device as with the back plates of Stegosaurus, and very handy for an animal that lived in equatorial extremes of climate.

Ouranosaurus

Classification Order Ornithischia, Suborder Ornithopoda
Age Cretaceous, 110 million years ago
Measurements Height 4 m (13.3 ft), length 7 m (23 ft)
Fossil sites North Africa
Notes Ouranosaurus, the 'brave reptile', was an iguanodontid that lived in an equatorial climate. The sail of skin stretched over backbone spines was probably used for temperature regulation.

The hadrosaurs

Hadrosaurs appeared in the middle of the Cretaceous period. The evidence points to them taking over ecological roles from iguanodontids wherever their geographical ranges overlapped, as in North America and Asia. They never reached western Europe, however, and the iguanodontids continued there until the end of the Age of Dinosaurs.

The typical hadrosaur body shape and size was similar to the iguanodontids. Their main innovations were in and on the head, and were concerned with food processing and social behaviour.

Anatosaurus was named 'duck reptile' for the duck-like bill which characterized the group. The front of the jaw formed a widely splayed 'beak', rather than the much narrower bill of the iguanodontids. Many rows of cheek teeth were cemented together to form rasping surfaces, for extra effectiveness in the never-ending task of crushing tough plant material. In fact, remains of the plants they ate – flowering and non-flowering trees and shrubs – have been preserved with one of the fossils.

The hands had only four fingers, the thumb (with its spike) having been lost. Hadrosaur hands were sometimes paddle-shaped, and together with the deep tail, this suggests that they could swim when necessary. Swimming was perhaps their only means of defence, because they otherwise seemed to lack armour or natural weapons.

RIGHT *Corythosaurus* was a large hadrosaur and displayed its group's tendency to develop crests and other headgear. The semicircular skull extension, formed from the nasal bones, contained a complicated arrangement of tubes and cavities, through which air could be drawn from the nostrils.

Anatosaurus

Classification Order Ornithischia, Suborder Ornithopoda
Age Late Cretaceous, 70 million years ago
Measurements Height about 3.6 m (12 ft), length 10 m (33 ft), weight 3 tonnes
Fossil sites North America
Notes *Anatosaurus* is one of the most common hadrosaur finds. Several whole animals have been pieced together, some with traces of skin covering the body – showing that the hands were webbed and could have been used for swimming.

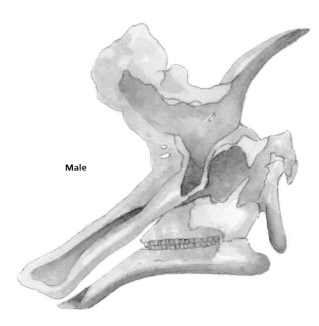

Male

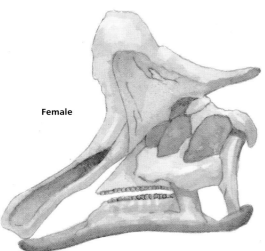

Female

LEFT Fossilized skulls of supposed male and female *Lambeosaurus* show that what biologists call 'secondary sexual characteristics' were present in these hadrosaurs. These types of dinosaurs were abundant and their fossils were once thought to represent more than a dozen different species. However, further work revealed that the crests were more likely to be from the males, females and juveniles of only three species.

Edmontosaurus

Classification Order Ornithischia, Suborder Ornithopoda
Age Late Cretaceous, 70 million years ago
Measurements Height 2.8 m (9.4 ft), length 10–13 m (33–42 ft)
Fossil sites North America
Notes *Edmontosaurus* is named for the place it was first found, Edmonton, Canada. The jaws of this hadrosaur formed the characteristic toothless 'duck-bill' at the front, while at the back were several hundred grinding teeth, arranged as flat rasping surfaces, that moved past each other as the animal chewed. These could certainly deal with tough vegetation. The animal also had paddle-like hands and a deep tail, perhaps for an escape swim when the land-based carnivorous dinosaurs threatened. These dinosaurs were social animals, nesting in colonies. Maybe they signalled to each other with an inflatable skin sack on the top of the nose, which could have made extremely loud sounds, similar to those made by the howler monkey's throat pouch.

Bumps on the head

The early hadrosaurs had various modifications to the front of the skull and nasal passages. Some had bumps on their noses, while others such as *Edmontosaurus* could probably inflate skin sacks, perhaps for visual display and vocalization, as in certain seals and some birds today.

In the best dinosaur tradition, these early adaptations were carried to extremes in later hadrosaurs. Strange crests, pipes, tubes and other projections appeared as headgear. These dinosaurs had big eyes and functional ear bones, so it is likely that the head adornments were used for visual and auditory signalling between individuals of a community.

One of the simpler designs was that of *Saurolophus*. It had a ridge on the top of the skull, and probably bore a fleshy, inflatable bag on the front of its face, connected to the nostrils. The most extreme development was found in *Parasaurolophus*, which had a long, curved crest on the top of its skull. This was hollow and connected to the nasal passages. There is good evidence that the crest was larger in males than in females of this dinosaur, and the likely conclusion is that this extraordinary 'topknot' was connected with courtship displays and/or territorial behaviour.

BELOW *Parasaurolophus* was one of the hadrosaur herbivores of the late Cretaceous period. Nasal passages passed from the nostrils, inside and up to the top of the crest, then down to the throat and lungs. This long tube may have been used as a 'trumpet' for vocal communication. The female skull is sectioned to show the shorter nasal passage which would have made a higher-pitched noise.

Saurolophus

Classification Order Ornithischia, Suborder Ornithopoda
Age Late Cretaceous, 70 million years ago
Measurements Height 4.2 m (14 ft), length 9–12 m (30–40 ft)
Fossil sites North America, Asia
Notes *Saurolophus* means 'ridged reptile', referring to the ridge of bone on the front of the face, which ended in a small spike at the top of the skull. Many hadrosaurs had these ridges or crests on their heads, which were probably used for social communication.

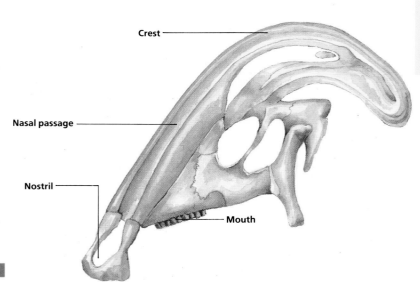

Crest

Nasal passage

Nostril

Mouth

Parasaurolophus

Classification Order Ornithischia, Suborder Ornithopoda

Age Late Cretaceous, 80 million years ago

Measurements Height 5.6 m (19 ft), length 10 m (33 ft)

Fossil sites North America

Notes *Parasaurolophus* means 'beside-ridged reptile'. It was a bipedal vegetarian, and member of the hadrosaur group. The extraordinary head ridge, much larger in the male than the female, was probably used as a social signalling device between members of the herd. It is thought that the hadrosaurs in general were noisy, social animals.

Maiasaura

Classification Order Ornithischia, Suborder Ornithopoda
Age Late Cretaceous, 80 million years ago
Measurements Height 2.4 m (8 ft), length 7 m (23 ft)
Fossil sites North America
Notes *Maiasaura*, 'good mother reptile', refers to the supposed behaviour of the parents, from evidence of eggs and baby hadrosaurs found fossilized in their nests. The babies were 50–100 cm (20–40 in) long, while larger young with worn teeth were found outside the nests. It seems that the animals nested in colonies, returning to the same site every year, and bringing their other youngsters. The mother laid 10–30 eggs, and she or some combination of adults raised the young and supplied them with food.

Iguanodon: safety in numbers?

Iguanodon and its dinosaur relatives were apparently fairly defenceless against the huge predators of their time, especially when compared to the horned and armoured dinosaurs. They had no plates or shields over their bodies, and apart from the relatively modest thumb spike, no weapons either. So did they rely on behavioural techniques for avoiding predation?

Safety in numbers is seen in the flocking and herding lifestyles of many birds and mammals today. Predators can be seen off by several large prey banding together. Even if the hunter is successful it can usually dispatch only one animal at a time, and when its appetite is satiated, the rest of the herd is safe. Indeed, by selecting old or sick members of the group, the carnivore acts as an agent of natural selection and picks out those 'leftover' individuals who are unlikely to pass their genes to the next generation.

It seems likely, then, that iguanodontids and hadrosaurs could have used these tactics for protection. At several sites, fossilized skeletons of many *Iguanodon* individuals have been discovered together – suggesting that they lived (and died) in herds. Further evidence comes from several parallel rows of fossilized *Iguanodon* footprints found in southern England. It may be that many animals walked across the mud together. Another clue comes from the communal nests of their close relatives, the hadrosaurs, in which case social behaviour could have been common to most members of the group.

ABOVE Most reptiles lay eggs, which are usually buried in a warm place. The young are left alone to hatch and fend for themselves. But crocodilians, despite their fierce nature, are very good parents. The mother watches over the buried eggs and digs the youngsters out when they call out after hatching. She carries them to a quiet 'nursery creek' and defends them until they are well grown. Various dinosaurs, such as *Maiasaura*, probably gave their youngsters a similar head start in life.

Good mothers – and fathers?

In 1978 a fossilized hadrosaur nesting site was discovered in Montana, North America. There are several nests containing eggs, hatchlings and youngsters of the dinosaur *Maiasaura*, which have revealed much about the behaviour of these animals. Interpretations of the remains so far give the following story.

It seems that the dinosaurs returned to the same colony site each year and rebuilt the nests. These were dug out of the sand by the female, using her hind feet. The nests are separated by a distance about equal to the length of an adult animal. This was presumably so that the mother had room to tend the nest while the eggs incubated, out of easy reach of her neighbours.

More than 20 eggs were laid, pointed ends down, and covered with sand. When the young hatched the mother brought food for the babies. The offspring stayed near the nest until quite well grown. This degree of parental care is rare in reptiles, but it is echoed by crocodiles and alligators which exhibit unexpected gentleness when handling their young, and utter selflessness in their protection.

What happened to the dinosaurs?

ABOVE The Age of
Mammals began shortly
after the beginning of the
Cenozoic period. Because
mammals are warm-
blooded and give birth to
live young, which they feed
with milk, they have been
successful all over the planet
– even in the coldest
regions.

Dinosaurs no longer thunder across the Earth's surface. If they did, we may not have evolved to the extent that we can produce books about them! They had all disappeared, every one, by about 65–64 million years ago.

The mass extinction happened quite suddenly, in terms of geological time, although newer evidence points to some groups tipping into decline beforehand. Nevertheless, after nearly 140 million years of successful evolution and diversification, they died out. The reasons have occupied hundreds of scientists from fields as varied as geology, animal pathology, astrophysics and statistical analysis, for many decades of our own minuscule time span. And there is still no single, firm, conclusive explanation – and there probably never will be.

Of the numerous theories put forward, some have been based on sound research. Others were less solidly founded, and a few may have been devised as publicity stunts. It is also strange that certain theories, no matter how well supported and thought through, seem to be difficult to accept in our current scientific climate.

In fact, there may well be some truth in more than one of the extinction notions. There is indeed evidence, to some degree, for most of them. Likewise, each has its difficulties.

BELOW A scene which has an unfamiliar ring: reptiles in the snow, which we do not recognize from today's world – because it is physiologically impossible. This small group of *iTriceratops* is pictured succumbing to the 'meteorite winter'. The dust cloud formed by the meteorite impact would have darkened the skies and cooled the Earth. Many reptiles, dependent as they are on the Sun for warmth, could not survive low temperatures. Or their food source – plants – could not photosynthesise in the gloom. The dinosaurs may have starved, or frozen, or both.

The reasons for extinction

The process of evolution depends on 'survival of the fittest'. Those that are not fit for the conditions in which they find themselves, become extinct. It seems to be the continuing fate of animal and plant species to evolve, diversify and then become extinct. It has happened to the vast majority of organisms that have ever lived on this Earth, and it will probably continue to do so; we humans are unlikely to be an exception to the rule.

The fossil record points to a 'background' rate of extinction, as small numbers of species disappear with continuing and monotonous regularity. However, at certain times, evidence shows that great numbers of species became extinct within a geologically short time – often resulting in great leaps forward thereafter, in evolutionary terms.

The sedimentary rocks that record the Earth's history change in character, as the conditions under which they were formed changed. These changes are reflected in the different names for the rock layers and their geological ages. The times of greatest extinction often coincide with boundaries between the major rock layers.

The fossil record suggests that at the Permian-Triassic boundary, 225 million years ago, as many as

70 per cent of marine organisms became extinct – the greatest mass extinction ever, overshadowing the dinosaurs' demise.

The Cretaceous-Tertiary boundary was when the dinosaurs themselves disappeared – and they were not alone. Numerous other major groups suffered with them in the worldwide event, including the marine ichthyosaurs and plesiosaurs, the flying pterosaurs, and many types of marine invertebrates – notably ammonites and calcareous plankton – as well as plenty of plant types. Yet there are many puzzles. Other groups of large reptiles, such as turtles and crocodiles, survived.

Regularity in the stars

Today we are constantly reminded of the increasing numbers of animals and plants disappearing from our world. The reasons for today's extinctions are not hard to find – they are caused by ourselves. But it is difficult to assess such causes in prehistoric times. Researchers have looked for a recurring cycle in the timing of past mass extinction events. Based on fossil records for marine organisms, a rough cycle of 26 million years has been found. The data do not fit perfectly, and there is great variation in the effects. But if there is a regular cycle, then presumably there must be a cause.

It seems likely that a cycle of such magnitude must be an extraterrestrial phenomenon. Astrophysicists have suggested there are periodic showers of comets hitting the Earth, and there is some geological evidence to support this theory. The showers may be caused by a periodic astronomical cycle, such as the orbit of vast unknown bodies, for example a twin star to our sun, or an unknown planet at the limits of our solar system. Alternatively, the showers may result from the movement of the entire solar system through dense dust clouds, encountered as it spirals through the Milky Way. Comet showers would have devastating effects on living things, but why specifically the dinosaurs and other groups were chosen, is even more subject to speculation.

Wandering continents

However, the cause may be closer to home. The continents move across the surface of the Earth on tectonic plates. This drifting is thought by some scientists to have been going on since the crust first cooled, and to have a cycle of about 440 million years. During this time the land masses on their plates come together to form a supercontinent, then split and move apart; the next cycle sees them moving close together again.

We know from the fossil record that the supercontinent of Pangaea formed 300–250 million years ago, and existed for some 100 million years. Since then the land masses have been moving towards their present positions. This continental drift would have great effects on sea levels and climate, and it may be echoed by the pattern of extinctions.

Climatic change

As we have seen, the initial success of the dinosaurs over other reptiles (and mammals) may have been due to the mild and stable climate during the later half of the Mesozoic era. The sediments laid down at that time were often those of desert sands, which suggests that much of the supercontinent was hot and dry. Pangaea was breaking up by the end of the era, and the continents were inching towards their present positions. We know that sea levels rose at this time and much of the land was flooded.

Today, we see that smaller land masses are cooler and moister than large ones. The subtropical vegetation in the centre of the huge supercontinent, on which the dinosaurs thrived, could therefore have been gradually replaced by more temperate plant cover, especially coniferous forests, as the land masses fragmented and the ocean winds and currents had a greater climatological effect. The climate might have become seasonal, with the warm summers and cold winters that we know today. Cold-blooded dinosaurs may not have been able to survive such variations.

Theories for the extinction of the dinosaurs fall into two main camps: those based on some sudden catastrophe, and those based on a (relatively) gradual change in conditions. The reason for their extinction may be easier to interpret if we knew whether they died out suddenly – the catastrophist approach – or more slowly, as in the gradualist theories.

The gradualist approach

When the dinosaurs disappeared, many plant and animal species disappeared at the same time. Marine plankton levels changed. Some flowering plants disappeared temporarily, to be replaced by ferns. Certain sea creatures had gone into significant decline before the end of the Cretaceous period.

Some researchers maintain that the dinosaurs remained diverse and numerous right up to the end. Others have found that in the last 10 million years or so of the Cretaceous, the number of taxonomic families decreased. They contend that only 12 species were left by its close, represented by virtually a 'handful' of fossil specimens. This apparent anomaly is due in part to the difficulties involved in accurately dating rocks and fossils, and of course to the notorious gaps in the fossil record when sedimentation and therefore fossilization, simply did not occur.

Some gradualists suggest that dinosaurs had all but exhausted their evolutionary potential. As we have seen, many of the late Cretaceous representatives were highly evolved, specialized creatures; for such 'hothouse flowers', sudden changes in environment would have had devastating effects. They simply could not survive in a changing world. Eventually they were to be superceded by the more adaptable mammals.

Extinction may have been caused by the ravages of disease. Indeed, dinosaur eggs from the time of the great extinction have been found with pathologically thin shells. Birds produce such eggs if they are poisoned, diseased or overheated. As the climate changed in favour of endothermic animals, the rapidly rising predation by egg-stealing nocturnal mammals may have overcome the dinosaurs.

ABOVE *Tsinatosaurus* was among the last of the dinosaurs. At the time of their disappearance, many dinosaur groups were developing evolutionarily eccentric characteristics such as ornate head appendages and complex armour. Perhaps some were too specialized to cope with catastrophe. Or they may have become susceptible to disease, as shown here.

A sudden catastrophe

The catastrophists favour a more traumatic explanation. Again, causes have been sought amongst the stars for such drastic changes. The sudden climatic changes caused by a meteorite collision with Earth, abnormal solar activity, or a supernova explosion resulting in deady cosmic rays, have been invoked to explain the extinctions.

The meteorite theory has some circumstantial evidence to support it. There are traces of the rare metal iridium in layers of clay at the Cretaceous-Tertiary boundary, found in rocks from various sites around the world. Iridium on Earth has only two sources. It is occasionally brought to the surface from the core, during unusual volcanic activity; or it is found in meteorites that fall from the sky. Calculating from the concentration of the element in these ancient clays, the iridium layer may have come from a meteorite some 10 km (6.5 miles) wide, which smashed into the Earth at this time. Often associated with the iridium layer in the clays are tiny glass spheres – and certain types of quartz are produced by heat, which could have been the result of such an impact.

The dust and debris hurled into the atmosphere following the impact would have blackened the skies for months, if not years. This is the same effect prophesied as the result of a nuclear war: climatically, the

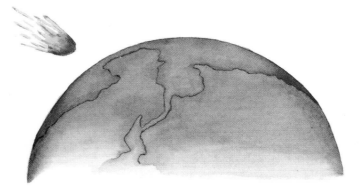

Meteorite approaches Earth

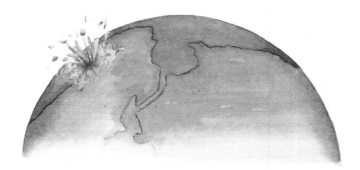

**Impact causes disintegration
of the meteorite and forms a
huge crater, like an atomic
explosion**

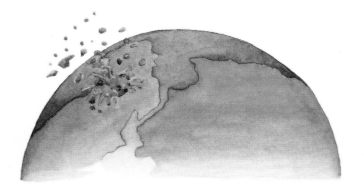

**Resulting debris flung into
the air**

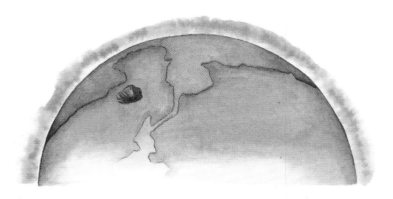

**Atmosphere distributes the
debris for many months**

'nuclear winter' and the 'meteorite winter' would have similar catastrophic results. The lack of sunlight would have had devastating effects on the plant life on land and in the sea. The Earth's surface temperature may have dropped drastically. Hence flowering plants were replaced by more shade-tolerant ferns. Even today, after volcanic activity, the bare ash is quickly colonized by ferns, and only later do flowering plants return.

Other possible results of a meteorite collision are that the gigantic impact heated the atmosphere to intolerable levels. This may have triggered a 'greenhouse effect'. Increased temperature of the Earth would explain thin-shelled eggs, and also the disappearance of creatures from the surface waters of the sea. (Deeper down, temperature changes would be less drastic.)

The meteorite impact may have released vast amounts of poisonous gases. These poisons may have killed animals directly, or they could have entered the food chain via plants.

If the meteorite fell in the sea, the resulting huge waves may have been responsible for mass deaths. There is some sedimentary evidence supporting this suggestion.

ABOVE One version of the catastrophic scenario for the end-of-Cretaceous mass extinction is a meteorite impact. An extraterrestrial body some 10km (6 miles) in diameter fell to Earth at colossal speed. Its impact, in the sea or perhaps on land, would have formed a huge crater and sent debris swirling into the atmosphere. The resulting cloud may have caused many months or years of darkness, reducing global temperatures.

Problems with meteorites

Many of the clues supporting a meteorite collision could, on the other hand, be explained by increased volcanic activity – for which there is also evidence. Another flaw in the meteorite theory is that many types of plants and animals were apparently unaffected by the catastrophe. And many of the groups that died out 65 million years ago had already definitely decreased, in variety and numbers, over a long period of time. Some had disappeared completely before the event, even if the dinosaurs had not. It is important to consider the total picture of life forms that existed at the time of the supposed meteorite impact: the patterns of extinction do not.

One of the thorniest parts of the whole problem is to account for why some land animals survived while others died, and why some sea creatures lived on while others perished. In particular, the survival of modern ectothermic reptiles is extremely difficult to explain. If the dinosaurs were ectothermic and they died because of drastic and widespread changes in temperature, how could today's reptiles have evolved?

And so, an ending

While the influence of extraterrestrial events in or near the solar system seems an unlikely explanation for the end of the Age of Dinosaurs, the possibility of a meteorite impact is not so difficult to imagine. There is much evidence in the rocks for this theory, and it fits with many of the effects on living things as we might picture them.

The devastation of plants, the base of the food web, by prolonged darkness caused by the dust cloud, would quickly affect the herbivores, and then the carnivores. The large reptiles of air, sea and land would have suffered also from temperature changes. As in today's post-nuclear war scenario, we can theorize that the survivors would be the less specialized opportunists, such as the insects and small mammals. However, the organisms that died out over the earlier period of time could not have been affected by the late appearance of a meteorite.

It may be that we are seeing the results of several events, which happened in the same few million years. Movements of continents, resulting climatic and sea level changes, and increased volcanic activity are normal events in the Earth's history. Conditions change, and evolution by natural selection picks the winners. The meteorite, if there was one, may well have been the final straw that broke the dinosaurs' back.

BELOW Whatever killed the dinosaurs changed the course of evolution. The chief survivors were endothermic opportunists. Mammals had been around nearly as long as the dinosaurs, but only after the demise of the 'terrible reptiles' did their opportunities arise.

Index

Picture Credits

t = top; b = bottom; l = left; r = right.

All illustrations by Elizabeth Sawyer (student from the School of Illustration, Bournemouth and Poole College of Art and Design), except those detailed below.

Danny McBride: pages 8, 11, 15
C.M. Dixon: page 13.
ET Archive: page 33 t.
GSF Picture Library/Dr B. Booth: pages 6, 14.
GSF Picture Library/R. Teede: page 70 t.
The Mansell Collection: page 72.
Jim Robins: pages 21, 35 tl, 38.
Graham Rosewarne: pages 24 t, 31, 48, 50, 51 t, 56 t, 61 b, 71 t.